IMPORTANT NOTICES AND DISCLAIMERS CONCERNII
NOTICE AND DISCLAIMER OF LIABILITY CONCERNING TH

MW00453023

NFPA® codes, standards, recommended practices, and guides ("NFPA Documents"), of which the document contained herein is one, are developed through a consensus standards development process approved by the American National Standards Institute. This process brings together volunteers representing varied viewpoints and interests to achieve consensus on fire and other safety issues. While the NFPA administers the process and establishes rules to promote fairness in the development of consensus, it does not independently test, evaluate, or verify the accuracy of any information or the soundness of any judgments contained in NFPA Documents.

The NFPA disclaims liability for any personal injury, property or other damages of any nature whatsoever, whether special, indirect, consequential or compensatory, directly or indirectly resulting from the publication, use of, or reliance on NFPA Documents. The NFPA also makes no guaranty or warranty as to the accuracy or completeness of any information published herein.

In issuing and making NFPA Documents available, the NFPA is not undertaking to render professional or other services for or on behalf of any person or entity. Nor is the NFPA undertaking to perform any duty owed by any person or entity to someone else. Anyone using this document should rely on his or her own independent judgment or, as appropriate, seek the advice of a competent professional in determining the exercise of reasonable care in any given circumstances.

The NFPA has no power, nor does it undertake, to police or enforce compliance with the contents of NFPA Documents. Nor does the NFPA list, certify, test, or inspect products, designs, or installations for compliance with this document. Any certification or other statement of compliance with the requirements of this document shall not be attributable to the NFPA and is solely the responsibility of the certifier or maker of the statement.

ISBN: 978-161665054-4 (Print)
ISBN: 978-161665055-1 (PDF)

12/09

12/09

NFPA® 45

Standard on

Fire Protection for Laboratories Using Chemicals

2011 Edition

This edition of NFPA 45, *Standard on Fire Protection for Laboratories Using Chemicals*, was prepared by the Technical Committee on Laboratories Using Chemicals and acted on by NFPA at its June Association Technical Meeting held June 7–10, 2010, in Las Vegas, NV. It was issued by the Standards Council on August 5, 2010, with an effective date of August 25, 2010, and supersedes all previous editions.

This edition of NFPA 45 was approved as an American National Standard on August 25, 2010.

Origin and Development of NFPA 45

The first edition of NFPA 45 was developed by the Technical Committee on Chemistry Laboratories. It was tentatively adopted at the 1974 NFPA Annual Meeting and was officially adopted at the 1975 NFPA Fall Meeting. The committee wishes to acknowledge that NFPA 45 is due in large part to the leadership and efforts of the late Russell H. Scott, who served as chairman of the committee during the planning and drafting stages of the first edition of NFPA 45. After the document had been in use for two years, the technical committee began an exhaustive review of the text; amendments were adopted for the 1982, 1986, and 1991 editions.

The 1996 edition of NFPA 45 included clarification on the scope and application of the standard as it applied to various types of educational, industrial, and medical laboratory facilities. Clarification of objectives was made to ensure a fire is contained to the room of origin. The requirements for maximum quantities of flammable and combustible liquids, construction, and fire protection in laboratory units were separated into two tables, one for sprinklered laboratory units and the other for nonsprinklered laboratory units. In addition, the committee revised the fire hazard classifications to recognize that clinical laboratories were using this standard as directed by NFPA 99, *Standard for Health Care Facilities*, and to identify that NFPA *101®*, *Life Safety Code®*, no longer addresses laboratory occupancies.

The 2000 edition of NFPA 45 included modified laboratory separation requirements, and nonsprinklered laboratories of Class A or B and Class C [over 929 m² (10,000 ft²)] were prohibited. Expanded requirements and advisory information for compressed and liquefied gases were added. Additional changes included modified laboratory ventilating systems and hood requirements. Average face velocity is used to determine the safe operating levels for hood exhaust systems. Changes were made to address the current industry trend in the utilization of VAV (Variable Air Volume) laboratory ventilation systems, which provide clear requirements for the containment of contaminants within the hood. The language was clarified regarding multiple or manifold exhaust ducts within buildings.

The 2004 edition of NFPA 45 included a new requirement that all new laboratories must be protected with automatic extinguishing systems. Pressurized liquid dispensing containers not previously recognized but indirectly prohibited because of quantity restrictions were defined, addressed, and regulated. Clarification of the scope was provided for labs containing the minimum quantity of either flammable and combustible liquids or gas that would qualify the lab for coverage under NFPA 45. Clarification was also made that the minimum quantity of gas does not include low-pressure utility gas in accordance with NFPA 54, *National Fuel Gas Code*. The 2004 edition included expanded advisory material on biological safety cabinets and recognition of listed Class II, Type B2 biological safety cabinets in lieu of chemical fume hoods under certain circumstances. All flammable and combustible liquids requirements were consolidated into one chapter. Requirements were incorporated to limit hazchem storage spill scenarios to less than 20 L (5 gal). Expanded requirements and advisory information were created for compressed and liquefied gases. Maximum quantity requirements were clarified for outside cylinder storage.

The 2011 edition of NFPA 45 includes major modifications to Chapters 4, 5, 9, 10, and 11 to modify the design, construction, and operational requirements for laboratories located in buildings over 1 story in height. Height restrictions were added for Class A and B laboratory units. The fire resistance rating of laboratory units, height restrictions, and quantities of hazardous materials were modified for laboratory units depending upon the height of the building containing the laboratories. Laboratories located in health care facilities previously covered by NFPA 99 were added to NFPA 45. Hazardous materials in storage or use in a laboratory work area that could present an explosion hazard were quantified. Requirements for the management of time-sensitive chemicals were clarified.

Technical Committee on Laboratories Using Chemicals

Andrew Minister, *Chair*
Battelle Northwest Laboratory, WA [U]

Richard R. Anderson, Anderson Risk Consultants, NJ [SE]

Raymond E. Arntson, Rayden Research, LLC, WI [SE]

William H. Barlen, Barlen and Associates, Inc., NJ [M]
Rep. Airgas, Inc. and Purification Technologies Inc.

Hal Cohen, HCC and Associates, Inc., DE [SE]

Michael F. Cooper, Harley Ellis Devereaux, MI [SE]

John L. Dembishack, III, Connecticut Department of Public Safety, CT [E]

William A. Eckholm, Firetrace International, AZ [M]

Kevin C. Gilkison, Labconco Corporation, MO [M]

Brian K. Goodman, Lawrence Livermore National Laboratory, CA [U]

Craig E. Hofmeister, The RJA Group, Inc., NC [SE]

Donald J. Kohn, Kohn Engineering, PA [SE]

Diane L. Kroll, U.S. Department of Veterans Affairs, MN [U]

John P. McCabe, U.S. National Institutes of Health, MD [E]

Robert Myers, Myers Safety Consultants (Amoco), GA [U]

Richard P. Palluzi, ExxonMobil Research & Engineering Company, NJ [U]

Paul Pelczynski, Siemens Building Technologies, Inc., IL [M]

Rudolph Poblete, Kewaunee Scientific Corporation, NC [M]

Michael J. Pokorny, Montgomery County, MD [E]

Ajay V. Prasad, Hughes Associates, Inc., MD [SE]

Peter Puhlick, University of Connecticut, CT [U]

David R. Quigley, BWXT Y-12, TN [U]

David S. Rausch, Phoenix Controls Corporation, MA [M]

James F. Riley, Riley Laboratory Consulting, LLC, GA [SE]

Michael W. St. Clair, Ostrander, OH [U]
Rep. NFPA Industrial Fire Protection Section

Steve Waller, CUH2A, Inc., NJ [SE]

Alternates

Jeremy R. Barrette, Phoenix Controls Corporation, MA [M]
(Alt. to D. S. Rausch)

Darren G. Cooke, University of Connecticut, CT [E]
(Alt. to J. L. Dembishack, III)

Samuel A. Denny, U.S. National Institutes of Health, MD [E]
(Alt. to J. P. McCabe)

Louis Hartman, Harley Ellis Devereaux, MI [SE]
(Alt. to M. F. Cooper)

Debra Sue Miller, The RJA Group, Inc., TX [SE]
(Alt. to C. E. Hofmeister)

Joseph J. Milligan, III, GlaxoSmithKline, A [U]
(Alt. to M. W. St. Clair)

Nonvoting

John Fresina, Bedford, MA
(Member Emeritus)

Norman V. Steere, Norman V. Steere & Associates, Inc., MN [SE]
(Member Emeritus)

Martha H. Curtis, NFPA Staff Liaison

This list represents the membership at the time the Committee was balloted on the final text of this edition. Since that time, changes in the membership may have occurred. A key to classifications is found at the back of the document.

NOTE: Membership on a committee shall not in and of itself constitute an endorsement of the Association or any document developed by the committee on which the member serves.

Committee Scope: This Committee shall have primary responsibility for documents for the prevention of loss of life and damage to property from fire and explosion in chemical laboratories.

Contents

NFPA 45

Standard on

Fire Protection for Laboratories Using Chemicals

2011 Edition

IMPORTANT NOTE: This NFPA document is made available for use subject to important notices and legal disclaimers. These notices and disclaimers appear in all publications containing this document and may be found under the heading "Important Notices and Disclaimers Concerning NFPA Documents." They can also be obtained on request from NFPA or viewed at www.nfpa.org/disclaimers.

NOTICE: An asterisk (*) following the number or letter designating a paragraph indicates that explanatory material on the paragraph can be found in Annex A.

Changes other than editorial are indicated by a vertical rule beside the paragraph, table, or figure in which the change occurred. These rules are included as an aid to the user in identifying changes from the previous edition. Where one or more complete paragraphs have been deleted, the deletion is indicated by a bullet (•) between the paragraphs that remain.

A reference in brackets [ ] following a section or paragraph indicates material that has been extracted from another NFPA document. As an aid to the user, the complete title and edition of the source documents for extracts in mandatory sections of the document are given in Chapter 2 and those for extracts in informational sections are given in Annex G. Extracted text may be edited for consistency and style and may include the revision of internal paragraph references and other references as appropriate. Requests for interpretations or revisions of extracted text shall be sent to the technical committee responsible for the source document.

Information on referenced publications can be found in Chapter 2 and Annex G.

Chapter 1 Administration

1.1 Scope.

1.1.1 This standard shall apply to laboratory buildings, laboratory units, and laboratory work areas whether located above or below grade in which chemicals, as defined, are handled or stored.

1.1.2 This standard shall not apply to the following:

(1)*Laboratories for which the following conditions apply:
  (a) Laboratory units that contain less than or equal to 4 L (1 gal) of flammable or combustible liquid
  (b) Laboratory units that contain less than 2.2 standard m³ (75 scf) of flammable gas, not including piped-in low-pressure utility gas installed in accordance with NFPA 54, *National Fuel Gas Code*
(2)*Laboratories that are pilot plants
(3) Laboratories that handle only chemicals with a hazard rating of 0 or 1, as defined by NFPA 704, *Standard System for the Identification of the Hazards of Materials for Emergency Response*, for all of the following: health, flammability, and instability

(4) Laboratories that are primarily manufacturing plants
(5) Incidental testing facilities
(6) Physical, electronic, instrument, laser, or similar laboratories that use chemicals only for incidental purposes, such as cleaning
(7)*Hazards associated with radioactive materials, as covered by NFPA 801, *Standard for Fire Protection for Facilities Handling Radioactive Materials*
(8) Laboratories that work only with explosive material, as covered by NFPA 495, *Explosive Materials Code*

1.1.3 This standard contains requirements, but not all-inclusive requirements, for handling and storage of chemicals where laboratory-scale operations are conducted and shall not cover the following:

(1) The special fire protection required when handling explosive materials *(See NFPA 495, Explosive Materials Code.)*
(2) The special fire protection required when handling radioactive materials

1.2 Purpose.

1.2.1 The purpose of this standard shall be to provide basic requirements for the protection of life and property through prevention and control of fires and explosions involving the use of chemicals in laboratory-scale operations.

1.2.2 This standard is designed to control hazards and protect personnel from the toxic, corrosive, or other harmful effects of chemicals to which personnel might be exposed as a result of fire or explosion.

1.2.3 The goal of this standard shall be to achieve a comprehensive laboratory fire prevention and protection program to prevent injury or death to occupants and emergency response personnel.

1.2.4 The objectives of this standard shall be as follows:

(1) Limit injury to the occupants at the point of fire origin
(2) Limit injury to emergency response personnel
(3) Limit property loss to a maximum of a single laboratory unit

1.2.5 It is not the objective of this standard to address financial losses such as business interruption or property loss when the loss of a laboratory unit is unacceptable.

1.3* Application.

1.3.1 The provisions of this document shall be considered necessary to provide a reasonable level of protection from loss of life and property from fire and explosion. They reflect situations and the state of the art prevalent at the time the standard was issued.

1.3.2 When interface with existing NFPA or other consensus codes and standards occurs, reference shall be made to the appropriate source in the text.

1.3.3 Due to the special nature of laboratories using chemicals, this standard modifies and supplements existing codes and standards so as to apply more specifically to buildings or portions of buildings devoted to laboratory-scale operations.

1.3.4 Where a construction or protection requirement of a governmental agency having jurisdiction is more stringent than a requirement in this standard, the more stringent requirement shall apply.

1.4 Retroactivity. The provisions of this standard reflect a consensus of what is necessary to provide an acceptable degree of protection from the hazards addressed in this standard at the time the standard was issued.

1.4.1 Unless otherwise specified, the provisions of this standard shall not apply to facilities, equipment, structures, or installations that existed or were approved for construction or installation prior to the effective date of the standard. Where specified, the provisions of this standard shall be retroactive.

1.4.2 In those cases where the authority having jurisdiction determines that the existing situation presents an unacceptable degree of risk, the authority having jurisdiction shall be permitted to apply retroactively any portions of this standard deemed appropriate.

1.4.3 The retroactive requirements of this standard shall be permitted to be modified if their application clearly would be impractical in the judgment of the authority having jurisdiction, and only where it is clearly evident that a reasonable degree of safety is provided.

1.5 Equivalency. Nothing in this standard is intended to prevent the use of systems, methods, or devices of equivalent or superior quality, strength, fire resistance, effectiveness, durability, and safety over those prescribed by this standard.

1.5.1 Technical documentation shall be submitted to the authority having jurisdiction to demonstrate equivalency.

1.5.2 The system, method, or device shall be approved for the intended purpose by the authority having jurisdiction.

Chapter 2   Referenced Publications

2.1 General. The documents or portions thereof listed in this chapter are referenced within this standard and shall be considered part of the requirements of this document.

2.2 NFPA Publications. National Fire Protection Association, 1 Batterymarch Park, Quincy, MA 02169-7471.

NFPA 10, *Standard for Portable Fire Extinguishers,* 2010 edition.

NFPA 11, *Standard for Low-, Medium-, and High-Expansion Foam,* 2010 edition.

NFPA 12, *Standard on Carbon Dioxide Extinguishing Systems,* 2008 edition.

NFPA 12A, *Standard on Halon 1301 Fire Extinguishing Systems,* 2009 edition.

NFPA 13, *Standard for the Installation of Sprinkler Systems,* 2010 edition.

NFPA 14, *Standard for the Installation of Standpipe and Hose Systems,* 2010 edition.

NFPA 15, *Standard for Water Spray Fixed Systems for Fire Protection,* 2007 edition.

NFPA 17, *Standard for Dry Chemical Extinguishing Systems,* 2009 edition.

NFPA 17A, *Standard for Wet Chemical Extinguishing Systems,* 2009 edition.

NFPA 25, *Standard for the Inspection, Testing, and Maintenance of Water-Based Fire Protection Systems,* 2011 edition.

NFPA 30, *Flammable and Combustible Liquids Code,* 2008 edition.

NFPA 33, *Standard for Spray Application Using Flammable or Combustible Materials,* 2011 edition.

NFPA 51, *Standard for the Design and Installation of Oxygen–Fuel Gas Systems for Welding, Cutting, and Allied Processes,* 2007 edition.

NFPA 54, *National Fuel Gas Code,* 2009 edition.

NFPA 55, *Compressed Gases and Cryogenic Fluids Code,* 2010 edition.

NFPA 58, *Liquefied Petroleum Gas Code,* 2011 edition.

NFPA 69, *Standard on Explosion Prevention Systems,* 2008 edition.

NFPA 70®, *National Electrical Code®,* 2011 edition.

NFPA 72®, *National Fire Alarm and Signaling Code,* 2010 edition.

NFPA 80, *Standard for Fire Doors and Other Opening Protectives,* 2010 edition.

NFPA 86, *Standard for Ovens and Furnaces,* 2011 edition.

NFPA 90A, *Standard for the Installation of Air-Conditioning and Ventilating Systems,* 2009 edition.

NFPA 91, *Standard for Exhaust Systems for Air Conveying of Vapors, Gases, Mists, and Noncombustible Particulate Solids,* 2010 edition.

NFPA 101®, *Life Safety Code®,* 2009 edition.

NFPA 495, *Explosive Materials Code,* 2010 edition.

NFPA 496, *Standard for Purged and Pressurized Enclosures for Electrical Equipment,* 2008 edition.

NFPA 704, *Standard System for the Identification of the Hazards of Materials for Emergency Response,* 2007 edition.

NFPA 750, *Standard on Water Mist Fire Protection Systems,* 2010 edition.

NFPA 801, *Standard for Fire Protection for Facilities Handling Radioactive Materials,* 2008 edition.

NFPA 1962, *Standard for the Inspection, Care, and Use of Fire Hose, Couplings, and Nozzles and the Service Testing of Fire Hose,* 2008 edition.

NFPA 2001, *Standard on Clean Agent Fire Extinguishing Systems,* 2008 edition.

2.3 Other Publications.

2.3.1 AIHA Publications. American Industrial Hygiene Association, 2700 Prosperity Avenue, Suite 250, Fairfax, VA 22031-4319.

ANSI/AIHA Z9.5, *Laboratory Ventilation,* 2003.

2.3.2 ANSI Publications. American National Standards Institute, Inc., 25 West 43rd Street, 4th Floor, New York, NY 10036.

ANSI Z535.1, *Safety Color Code,* 2006.

ANSI Z535.2, *Environmental and Facility Safety Signs,* 2007.

ANSI Z535.3, *Criteria for Safety Symbols,* 2007.

ANSI Z535.4, *Product Safety Signs and Labels,* 2007.

2.3.3 ASME Publications. American Society of Mechanical Engineers, Three Park Avenue, New York, NY 10016-5990.

ASME *Boiler and Pressure Vessel Code,* Section VIII, 2007.

2.3.4 ASTM Publications. ASTM International, 100 Barr Harbor Drive, P.O. Box C700, West Conshohocken, PA 19428-2959.

ASTM D 5, *Standard Test Method of Penetration of Bituminous Materials,* 2006.

ASTM E 84, *Standard Test Method for Surface Burning Characteristics of Building Materials,* 2010.

2.3.5 NSF Publications. NSF International, P.O. Box 130140, 789 N. Dixboro Road, Ann Arbor, MI 48113-0140.

NSF/ANSI 49, *Class II (Laminar Flow) Biosafety Cabinetry,* 2007.

2.3.6 UL Publications. Underwriters Laboratories, Inc. 333 Pfingsten Road, Northbrook, IL 60062-2096.

ANSI/UL 723, *Standard for Test for Surface Burning Characteristics of Building Materials*, 2008.

UL 1275, *Standard for Flammable Liquid Cabinets*, 2005.

2.3.7 Other Publications.

Merriam-Webster's Collegiate Dictionary, 11th edition, Merriam-Webster, Inc., Springfield, MA, 2003.

2.4 References for Extracts in Mandatory Sections.
NFPA 54, *National Fuel Gas Code*, 2009 edition.
NFPA 99, *Standard for Health Care Facilities*, 2005 edition.
NFPA *101®, Life Safety Code®*, 2009 edition.
NFPA 5000®, Building Construction and Safety Code®, 2009 edition.

Chapter 3 Definitions

3.1 Definitions. The definitions contained in this chapter shall apply to the terms used in this standard. Where terms are not defined in this chapter or within another chapter, they shall be defined using their ordinarily accepted meanings within the context in which they are used. *Merriam-Webster's Collegiate Dictionary*, 11th edition, shall be the source for the ordinarily accepted meaning.

3.2 NFPA Official Definitions.

3.2.1* Approved. Acceptable to the authority having jurisdiction.

3.2.2* Authority Having Jurisdiction (AHJ). An organization, office, or individual responsible for enforcing the requirements of a code or standard, or for approving equipment, materials, an installation, or a procedure.

3.2.3 Labeled. Equipment or materials to which has been attached a label, symbol, or other identifying mark of an organization that is acceptable to the authority having jurisdiction and concerned with product evaluation, that maintains periodic inspection of production of labeled equipment or materials, and by whose labeling the manufacturer indicates compliance with appropriate standards or performance in a specified manner.

3.2.4* Listed. Equipment, materials, or services included in a list published by an organization that is acceptable to the authority having jurisdiction and concerned with evaluation of products or services, that maintains periodic inspection of production of listed equipment or materials or periodic evaluation of services, and whose listing states that either the equipment, material, or service meets appropriate designated standards or has been tested and found suitable for a specified purpose.

3.2.5 Shall. Indicates a mandatory requirement.

3.2.6 Should. Indicates a recommendation or that which is advised but not required.

3.2.7 Standard. A document, the main text of which contains only mandatory provisions using the word "shall" to indicate requirements and which is in a form generally suitable for mandatory reference by another standard or code or for adoption into law. Nonmandatory provisions shall be located in an appendix or annex, footnote, or fine-print note and are not to be considered a part of the requirements of a standard.

3.3 General Definitions.

3.3.1 Apparatus. Furniture, chemical fume hoods, centrifuges, refrigerators, and commercial or made-on-site equipment used in a laboratory.

3.3.2 Auxiliary Air. Supply or supplemental air delivered near the outside face of a chemical fume hood to reduce room air consumption.

3.3.3 Baffle. An object placed in an appliance to change the direction of or to retard the flow of air, air–gas mixtures, or flue gases. [54, 2009]

3.3.4* Biological Safety Cabinet. A ventilated cabinet for personnel, product, and environmental protection having an open front with inward airflow for personnel protection, downward HEPA-filtered laminar airflow for product protection, and HEPA-filtered exhausted air for environmental protection.

3.3.5 Business Occupancy. See 3.3.45.1.

3.3.6 Bypass. An airflow-compensating opening that maintains a relatively constant volume exhaust through a chemical fume hood regardless of sash position, serving to limit the maximum face velocity as the sash is lowered.

3.3.7 Canopy Hood. A suspended ventilating device used only to exhaust heat, water vapor, odors, and other nonhazardous materials. This is not a chemical fume hood and generally is not effective for exhausting toxic or flammable materials.

3.3.8* Chemical. A substance with one or more of the following hazard ratings as defined in NFPA 704, *Standard System for the Identification of the Hazards of Materials for Emergency Response:* Health — 2, 3, or 4; Flammability — 2, 3, or 4; Instability — 2, 3, or 4. *(See also Section B.2.)*

3.3.9* Chemical Fume Hood. A ventilated enclosure designed to contain and exhaust fumes, gases, vapors, mists, and particulate matter generated within the hood interior.

3.3.10 Combustible Liquid. A liquid that has a closed-cup flash point at or above 37.8°C (100°F).

3.3.11 Compressed Gas Cylinder. Any portable pressure vessel of 45.4 kg (100 lb) water capacity or less designed to contain a gas or liquid that is authorized for use at gauge pressures over 276 kPa (40 psi) at 21°C (70°F) by the U.S. Department of Transportation (DOT) or Transport Canada (T.C.).

3.3.12* Cryogenic Fluid. Substance that exists only in the vapor phase above −73°C (−99°F) at one atmosphere pressure and that is handled, stored, and used in the liquid state at temperatures at or below −73°C (−99°F) while at any pressure.

3.3.13 Deflector Vane. An airfoil-shaped vane along the bottom of the hood face that directs incoming air across the work surface to the lower baffle opening. The opening between the work surface and the deflector vane is open even with the sash fully closed.

3.3.14 Educational Laboratory Unit. A laboratory unit that is used for educational purposes through the twelfth grade by six or more persons for four or more hours per day or more than 12 hours per week.

3.3.15 Educational Occupancy. See 3.3.45.2.

3.3.16 Exit Access Corridor. A corridor used as exit access that leads to an exit that is separated from other parts of the building by walls.

3.3.17 Explosive Material. Any explosive, blasting agent, emulsion explosive, water gel, or detonator.

3.3.18* Face (of hood). The hood opening or the plane of the inside surface of the sash.

3.3.19 Face Velocity. The rate of flow or velocity of air moving into the chemical fume hood entrance or face, as measured at the plane of the chemical fume hood face.

3.3.20 Fire Separation. A horizontal or vertical fire resistance–rated assembly of materials that have protected openings and are designed to restrict the spread of fire.

3.3.21 Flammable Gas. Any substance that exists in the gaseous state at normal atmospheric temperature and pressure and is capable of being ignited and burned when mixed with the proper proportions of air, oxygen, or other oxidizers. [**99,** 2005]

3.3.22 Flammable Liquid. A liquid that has a closed-cup flash point that is below 37.8°C (100°F) and a maximum vapor pressure of 2068 mm Hg (absolute pressure of 40 psi) at 37.8°C (100°F).

3.3.23* Flammable Solid. A solid, other than a blasting agent or explosive, that is liable to cause fire through friction, absorption of moisture, spontaneous chemical change, or retained heat from manufacturing or processing, or that can be ignited readily and when ignited, burns so vigorously and persistently as to create a serious hazard.

3.3.24 Flash Point. The minimum temperature at which a liquid or a solid emits vapor sufficient to form an ignitible mixture with air near the surface of the liquid or the solid.

3.3.25* Health Care Facilities. Buildings or portions of buildings in which medical, dental, psychiatric, nursing, obstetrical, or surgical care is provided. [**99,** 2005]

3.3.26 Health Care Occupancy. See 3.3.45.3.

3.3.27 Hood Interior. The volume enclosed by the side, back, and top enclosure panels, the work surface, the access opening (called the face), the sash or sashes, and the exhaust plenum, including the baffle system for airflow distribution.

3.3.28 Incidental Testing Facility. An area within a production facility set aside for the purpose of conducting in-process control tests that are related to the production process.

3.3.29 Industrial Occupancy. See 3.3.45.4.

3.3.30* Inside Liquid Storage Area. A room or building used for the storage of liquids in containers or portable tanks, separated from other types of occupancies.

3.3.31 Instructional Laboratory Unit. A laboratory unit used for education past the 12th grade and before post-college graduate-level instruction for the purposes of instruction of six or more persons for four or more hours per day or more than 12 hours per week. Experiments and tests conducted in instructional laboratory units are under the direct supervision of an instructor. Laboratory units used for graduate or post-graduate research are not to be considered instructional laboratory units.

3.3.32 Laboratory. A facility where the containers used for reactions, transfers, and other handling of chemicals are designed to be easily and safely manipulated by one person. A laboratory is a workplace where chemicals are used or synthesized on a nonproduction basis.

3.3.33 Laboratory Building. A structure consisting wholly or principally of one or more laboratory units.

3.3.34 Laboratory Equipment. See 3.3.1, Apparatus.

3.3.35 Laboratory Scale. Work with chemicals in which the containers used for reactions, transfers, and other handling of chemicals are designed to be easily and safely manipulated by one person.

3.3.36 Laboratory Unit. An enclosed space used for experiments or tests. A laboratory unit can include offices, lavatories, and other incidental contiguous rooms maintained for or used by laboratory personnel, and corridors within the unit. It can contain one or more separate laboratory work areas. It can be an entire building. A laboratory unit is classified as A, B, C, or D in accordance with Section 4.2. *(See also Annex D.)*

3.3.37 Laboratory Unit Separation. All walls, partitions, floors, and ceilings, including openings in them, that separate a laboratory unit from adjoining areas.

3.3.38* Laboratory Work Area. A room or space for testing, analysis, research, instruction, or similar activities that involve the use of chemicals.

3.3.39 Laminar Flow Cabinet. A ventilated, partially enclosed cabinet primarily intended to provide filtered airflow over the work surface by use of laminar airflow methods.

3.3.40 Lecture Bottle. A small compressed gas cylinder up to a size of approximately 5 cm × 33 cm (2 in. × 13 in.).

3.3.41 Liquefied Gas Cylinder. A compressed gas cylinder used for liquefied gas.

3.3.42 Liquid. A material that has a fluidity greater than that of 300 penetration asphalt when tested in accordance with ASTM D 5, *Standard Test Method of Penetration of Bituminous Materials.* Unless otherwise specified, the term *liquid* includes both flammable and combustible liquids.

3.3.43 Maximum Allowable Working Pressure. The maximum gauge pressure permissible at the top of completed equipment, a container, or a vessel in its operating position for a design temperature.

3.3.44 Non-Laboratory Area. Any space within a building not included in a laboratory unit. *(See also 3.3.36.)*

3.3.45 Occupancy.

3.3.45.1 *Business Occupancy.* An occupancy used for the transaction of business other than mercantile. [**5000,** 2009]

3.3.45.2* *Educational Occupancy.* An occupancy used for educational purposes through the 12th grade by six or more persons for 4 or more hours per day or more than 12 hours per week.

3.3.45.3 *Health Care Occupancy.* An occupancy used for purposes of medical or other treatment or care of four or more persons where such occupants are mostly incapable of self-preservation due to age, physical or mental disability, or because of security measures not under the occupants' control. [**5000,** 2009]

3.3.45.4* *Industrial Occupancy.* An occupancy in which products are manufactured or in which processing, assembling, mixing, packaging, finishing, decorating, or repair operations are conducted. [**5000,** 2009]

3.3.46 Open Plan Building. A building having rooms, spaces, and corridors delineated by tables, chairs, desks, bookcases, counters, low-height partitions, floor patterns, or any similar finishes or furnishings.

3.3.47 Organic Peroxide. Any organic compound having a double oxygen or peroxy (-O-O-) group in its chemical structure.

3.3.48* Oxidizer. Any material that readily yields oxygen or other oxidizing gas, or that readily reacts to promote or initiate combustion of combustible materials.

3.3.49 Pilot Plant. An experimental assembly of equipment for exploring process variables or for producing semicommercial quantities of materials.

3.3.50 Pressurized Liquid Dispensing Container (PLDC). DOT-, United Nations- (UN-), or ASME-approved containers which are designed for the pressure dispensing of liquids at the specified maximum allowable working pressure of the container.

3.3.51 Pyrophoric Gas. A gas that will spontaneously ignite in air at or below a temperature of 54.4°C (130°F).

3.3.52 Qualified Person. A person who, by possession of a recognized degree, certificate, professional standing, or skill, and who, by knowledge, training, and experience, has demonstrated the ability to deal with problems relating to a particular subject matter, work, or project.

3.3.53 Reactive Material. A material that, by itself, is readily capable of detonation, explosive decomposition, or explosive reaction at normal or elevated temperatures and pressures. *(See B.2.5 for definitions of Instability 2, 3, or 4.)*

3.3.54 Refrigerating Equipment. Any mechanically operated equipment used for storing materials below normal ambient temperature, including refrigerators, freezers, and similar equipment. *(See 12.2.2 and A.12.2.2.2.)*

3.3.55 Safety Can. A listed container, of not more than 18.9 L (5 gal) capacity, having a spring-closing lid and spout cover and so designed that it will safely relieve internal pressure when subjected to fire exposure.

3.3.56 Sash. A movable panel or panels set in the hood entrance. *(See C.5.1.)*

3.3.57* Storage Cabinet. A cabinet for the storage of flammable and combustible liquids constructed in accordance with Section 9.5 of NFPA 30, *Flammable and Combustible Liquids Code.*

3.3.58 Street Floor. A story or floor level accessible from the street or from outside the building at ground level, with the floor level at the main entrance located not more than three risers above or below ground level, and arranged and utilized to qualify as the main floor. [**101,** 2009]

3.3.59* Unattended Laboratory Operation. A laboratory procedure or operation at which there is no person present who is knowledgeable regarding the operation and emergency shutdown procedures.

Chapter 4   Laboratory Unit Hazard Classification

4.1 General.

4.1.1 This chapter shall classify laboratory units based on the amount of flammable and combustible liquids in use within the unit.

4.1.2 This chapter also shall define the existence of an explosion hazard in a laboratory unit or in a laboratory work area.

4.1.3 This chapter shall further define limitations on instructional laboratory units.

4.2 Laboratory Unit Fire Hazard Classification.

4.2.1* Classifications.

4.2.1.1 Laboratory units shall be classified as Class A (high fire hazard), Class B (moderate fire hazard), Class C (low fire hazard), or Class D (minimal fire hazard), according to the quantities of flammable and combustible liquids specified in Table 10.1.1(a) and Table 10.1.1(b).

4.2.2 Additional Requirements for Educational and Instructional Laboratory Units.

4.2.2.1 Instructional laboratory units shall be classified as Class C or Class D laboratory units.

4.2.2.2 Educational laboratory units shall be classified as Class D or shall be limited to 50 percent of the flammable and combustible liquids quantity for Class C laboratory units presented in Table 10.1.1(a) and Table 10.1.1(b).

4.3 Laboratory Work Area and Laboratory Unit Explosion Hazard Classification.

4.3.1* A laboratory work area shall be considered to contain an explosion hazard if an explosion of quantities or concentrations of materials could result in serious or fatal injuries to personnel within that laboratory work area. Such quantities or concentrations include, but are not limited to, the following (*see Annex C*):

(1) Storage of greater than 0.45 kg (1 lb) of materials with an instability hazard rating of 4 *(see B.2.5)*
(2) Use or formation of greater than 0.11 kg (0.25 lb) of materials with an instability hazard rating of 4 *(see B.2.5)*
(3)*Presence of highly exothermic reactions in glass or open reaction vessels involving more than 10 g (0.35 oz) of materials such as polymerizations, oxidations, nitrations, peroxidations, hydrogenations, or organo-metallic reactions
(4) Use or formation in glass or open reaction vessels involving more than 10 g (0.35 oz) of materials whose chemical structures indicate a potential hazard, but whose properties have not been established, such as salts of alkenes, triple bonds, epoxy radicals, nitro and nitroso compounds, and peroxides
(5) Presence of high-pressure reactions *(see Figure C.4.5)*
(6) Other explosion hazards as determined by a qualified person

4.3.2 A laboratory unit shall not be considered to contain an explosion hazard unless a laboratory work area within that unit contains an explosion hazard great enough to cause major property damage or serious injury outside that laboratory work area.

Chapter 5   Laboratory Unit Design and Construction

5.1 Laboratory Unit Enclosure.

5.1.1 The required construction of laboratory units shall be in accordance with Table 5.1.1.

5.1.2 The construction requirements shall be the minimum permitted and shall not exclude the use of construction with greater fire resistance.

Table 5.1.1 Separation Requirements and Height Allowances for Laboratory Units

Laboratory Unit[a]	Area of Lab Unit	Fire Separation[b]	Permitted Stories Above Grade
A	≤929 m² (≤10,000 ft²)	2 hours	1–3[c]
	>929 m² (>10,000 ft²)	Not permitted[d]	
B	≤929 m² (≤10,000 ft²)	1 hour	1–3[c]
	≤929 m² (≤10,000 ft²)	2 hours	4–6[c]
	>929 m² (>10,000 ft²)	Not permitted[d]	
C	Any size	Not required	1–3
	Any size	1 hour	4–6
	Any size	2 hours	Over 6
D	Any size	Not required	No limit

[a]Refer to Table 10.1.1 for laboratory unit classification.
[b]Separation in this table refers to separation from laboratory unit(s) to non-laboratory areas and/or separations from laboratory unit(s) of equal or lower hazard classification.
[c]Not allowed in structures below grade.
[d]Labs of this classification and size are not permitted.

5.1.3 Regardless of the construction and fire protection requirements for laboratory units that are specified in Table 5.1.1, laboratory units in educational occupancies shall be separated from non-laboratory areas by 1-hour construction.

5.1.4 Table 5.1.1 shall pertain to laboratory units protected by automatic sprinkler systems in accordance with NFPA 13, *Standard for the Installation of Sprinkler Systems.* Where water will create a serious fire or personnel hazard, a suitable nonwater automatic extinguishing system shall be permitted to be an acceptable substitute for sprinklers.

5.1.5 Penetrations through fire-rated floor/ceiling, floor, and wall assemblies shall be protected in accordance with NFPA *101, Life Safety Code.*

5.1.6 Floors shall be sealed to prevent liquid leakage to lower floors.

5.1.7 Floor openings, floor penetrations, and floor firestop systems shall be sealed or curbed to prevent liquid leakage to lower floors.

5.1.8 Door assemblies in required 1-hour-rated fire separations shall be ¾-hour rated. Door assemblies in required 2-hour-rated fire separations shall be 1½-hour rated.

5.1.9 Window assemblies shall be permitted in fire-rated wall assemblies having a required fire resistance rating of 1 hour or less.

5.1.9.1 Window assemblies shall be of an approved type and shall have a fire protection rating in accordance with NFPA *101, Life Safety Code.*

5.1.9.2 Fire window assemblies shall be installed in accordance with NFPA 80, *Standard for Fire Doors and Other Opening Protectives.*

5.1.10* Openings in fire-rated floor/ceiling and wall assemblies for air-handling ductwork or air movement shall be protected in accordance with NFPA 90A, *Standard for the Installation of Air-Conditioning and Ventilating Systems.*

5.2 Maximum Area of Laboratory Units. The maximum area of a laboratory unit shall be determined by the fire hazard classification and the construction of the laboratory unit, as shown in Table 5.1.1.

5.3 Requirements for Life Safety. Life safety features for laboratory buildings, laboratory units, and laboratory work areas shall comply with NFPA *101, Life Safety Code,* unless otherwise modified by other provisions of this standard.

5.3.1 Class A, B, and C laboratory units shall be classified as industrial occupancies in accordance with NFPA *101, Life Safety Code.*

5.3.2 Educational laboratory units shall be classified as educational occupancies in accordance with NFPA *101, Life Safety Code.*

5.3.3 Instructional laboratory units and Class D laboratories shall be classified as business occupancies in accordance with NFPA *101, Life Safety Code.*

5.3.4 Life safety requirements for instructional laboratory units for past the 12th grade, and for Class D laboratories located in facilities classified as business occupancies, shall be in accordance with the requirements for business occupancies of NFPA *101, Life Safety Code.*

5.4 Means of Access to an Exit.

5.4.1* A second means of access to an exit shall be provided from a laboratory work area if any of the following situations exist:

(1) A laboratory work area contains an explosion hazard located so that an incident would block escape from or access to the laboratory work area.
(2) A laboratory work area within a Class A laboratory unit exceeds 46.5 m² (500 ft²).
(3) A laboratory work area within a Class B, Class C, or Class D laboratory unit exceeds 93 m² (1000 ft²).
(4) A hood in a laboratory work area is located adjacent to the primary means of exit access.
(5) A compressed gas cylinder larger than lecture bottle size [approximately 5 cm × 33 cm (2 in. × 13 in.)] is located such that it could prevent safe egress in the event of accidental release of cylinder contents.
(6) A cryogenic container is located such that it could prevent safe egress in the event of accidental release of container contents.

5.4.2 The required exit access doors of all laboratory work areas within Class A or Class B laboratory units shall swing in the direction of exit travel.

5.4.3* The required exit access doors of all laboratory work areas within Class C or Class D laboratory units shall be permitted to swing against the direction of exit travel or shall be permitted to be a horizontal sliding door complying with NFPA *101, Life Safety Code.*

5.4.4 Emergency lighting facilities shall be provided for any laboratory work area requiring a second means of access to an exit, in accordance with 5.4.1.

5.4.5 Emergency lighting in laboratory work areas and exits shall be installed in accordance with Section 7.9, Emergency Lighting, of NFPA *101, Life Safety Code.*

5.5* Furniture, Casework, and Equipment. Furniture, casework, and equipment in laboratory units shall be arranged so that means of access to an exit can be reached easily from any point.

5.6 Electrical Installation. All electrical installations, including wiring and appurtenances, apparatus, lighting, signal systems, alarm systems, remote control systems, or parts thereof, shall comply with *NFPA 70, National Electrical Code.*

5.6.1 Electrical receptacles, switches, and controls shall be located so as not to be subject to liquid spills.

5.6.2 Laboratory work areas, laboratory units, and chemical fume hood interiors shall be considered as unclassified electrically with respect to Article 500 of *NFPA 70, National Electrical Code.*

Exception: Under some conditions of hazard, it could be necessary to classify a laboratory work area, or a part thereof, as a hazardous location, for the purpose of designating the electrical installations. [See 10.5.5 (electric motors) and 12.2.2.2 (refrigerators).]

Chapter 6   Fire Protection

6.1 General.

6.1.1 All laboratory units shall be provided with fire protection appropriate to the fire hazard, as follows:

(1) Portable fire extinguishers *(see Section 6.4)*
(2) Fire alarm systems *(see Section 6.5)*
(3) Evacuation and emergency plans *(see 6.6.3)*

6.1.2 In addition to the fire protection specified in 6.1.1, laboratory units under some conditions shall be provided with automatic extinguishing systems *(see Section 6.2)* and inside standpipe and hose systems *(see Section 6.3).*

6.2 Automatic Fire Extinguishing Systems.

6.2.1 Automatic Sprinkler Systems.

6.2.1.1 Automatic sprinkler system protection shall be required for all new laboratories in accordance with the following:

(1) Automatic sprinkler system protection for Class A and Class B laboratories shall be in accordance with NFPA 13, *Standard for the Installation of Sprinkler Systems,* for ordinary hazard (Group 2) occupancies.
(2) Automatic sprinkler system protection for Class C and Class D laboratories shall be in accordance with NFPA 13, *Standard for the Installation of Sprinkler Systems,* for ordinary hazard (Group 1) occupancies.

6.2.1.2 Fire sprinklers in laboratory units shall be the quick-response (QR) sprinkler type installed in accordance with NFPA 13, *Standard for the Installation of Sprinkler Systems.*

6.2.1.3 Automatic sprinkler systems shall be regularly inspected, tested, and maintained in accordance with NFPA 25, *Standard for the Inspection, Testing, and Maintenance of Water-Based Fire Protection Systems.*

6.2.2 Other Automatic Extinguishing Systems. Where required or used in place of automatic sprinkler systems, special hazard extinguishing systems and nonwater automatic extinguishing systems shall be designed, installed, and maintained in accordance with the following standards, as applicable:

(1) NFPA 11, *Standard for Low-, Medium-, and High-Expansion Foam*
(2) NFPA 12, *Standard on Carbon Dioxide Extinguishing Systems*
(3) NFPA 12A, *Standard on Halon 1301 Fire Extinguishing Systems*
(4) NFPA 15, *Standard for Water Spray Fixed Systems for Fire Protection*
(5) NFPA 17, *Standard for Dry Chemical Extinguishing Systems*
(6) NFPA 17A, *Standard for Wet Chemical Extinguishing Systems*
(7) NFPA 69, *Standard on Explosion Prevention Systems*
(8) NFPA 750, *Standard on Water Mist Fire Protection Systems*
(9) NFPA 2001, *Standard on Clean Agent Fire Extinguishing Systems*

6.2.3* Discharge. The discharge of an automatic fire-extinguishing system shall activate an audible fire alarm system on the premises.

6.3 Standpipe and Hose Systems.

6.3.1* In all laboratory buildings that are two or more stories above or below the grade level (level of exit discharge), standpipes shall be installed in accordance with NFPA 14, *Standard for the Installation of Standpipe and Hose Systems.*

6.3.2 Standpipe systems shall be regularly inspected, tested, and maintained in accordance with NFPA 25, *Standard for the Inspection, Testing, and Maintenance of Water-Based Fire Protection Systems.*

6.3.3 Hose lines shall be of an approved type and shall be tested and maintained in accordance with NFPA 1962, *Standard for the Inspection, Care, and Use of Fire Hose, Couplings, and Nozzles and the Service Testing of Fire Hose.*

6.4 Portable Fire Extinguishers.

6.4.1 Portable fire extinguishers shall be installed, located, and maintained in accordance with NFPA 10, *Standard for Portable Fire Extinguishers.*

6.4.2 For purposes of sizing and placement of fire extinguishers for Class B fires *(see Table 6.3.1.1 of NFPA 10, Standard for Portable Fire Extinguishers),* Class A laboratory units shall be rated as extra (high) hazard, and Class B, Class C, and Class D laboratory units shall be rated as ordinary (moderate) hazard.

6.5 Fire Alarm Systems.

6.5.1 Fire alarm systems, where provided, shall be installed and maintained in accordance with *NFPA 72, National Fire Alarm and Signaling Code.*

6.5.2 Class A and Class B laboratory units shall have a manual fire alarm system installed and maintained in accordance with *NFPA 72, National Fire Alarm and Signaling Code.*

6.5.3 The fire alarm system, where provided, shall be designed so that all personnel endangered by the fire condition or a contingent condition shall be alerted.

6.5.4 The fire alarm system shall alert local emergency responders or the public fire department.

6.6 Fire Prevention.

6.6.1 Fire Prevention Procedures.

6.6.1.1 Fire prevention procedures shall be established.

6.6.1.2 Certain critical areas shall require special consideration, including, but not limited to, the following:

(1) Handling and storage of chemicals, flammable and combustible liquids, and gases
(2) Open flame and spark-producing equipment work permit system
(3) Arrangements and use of portable electrical cords
(4) Smoking area controls

6.6.2* Maintenance Procedures. Maintenance procedures shall be established.

6.6.3* Emergency Plans.

6.6.3.1 Plans for laboratory emergencies shall be developed, which shall include the following:

(1) Alarm activation
(2) Evacuation and building re-entry procedures
(3) Shutdown procedures or applicable emergency operations for equipment, processes, ventilation devices, and enclosures
(4) Fire-fighting operations
(5)*Non-fire hazards
(6) Information as required by the AHJ to allow the emergency responders to develop response tactics

6.6.3.2* Procedures for extinguishing clothing fires shall be established.

Chapter 7 Explosion Hazard Protection

7.1 General.

7.1.1 When a laboratory work area or a laboratory unit is considered to contain an explosion hazard, as defined in 4.3.1 and 4.3.2, appropriate protection shall be provided for the occupants of the laboratory work area, the laboratory unit, adjoining laboratory units, and non-laboratory areas. *(See Annex C for further information.)*

7.1.2 Protection shall be provided by one or more of the following:

(1) Limiting amounts of flammable or reactive chemicals or chemicals with unknown characteristics used in or exposed by experiments
(2) Special preventive or protective measures for the reactions, equipment, or materials themselves (e.g., high-speed fire detection with deluge sprinklers, explosion-resistant equipment or enclosures, explosion suppression, and explosion venting directed to a safe location)
(3) Explosion-resistant walls or barricades around the laboratory work area containing the explosion hazard *(see Section 7.2)*
(4) Remote control of equipment to minimize personnel exposure
(5) Sufficient deflagration venting in outside walls to maintain the integrity of the walls separating the hazardous laboratory work area or laboratory unit from adjoining areas
(6) Conducting experiments in a detached or isolated building, or outdoors

7.2 Explosion-Resistant Construction. When explosion-resistant construction is used, adequately designed explosion resistance shall be achieved by the use of one of the following methods:

(1) Reinforced concrete walls
(2) Reinforced and fully grouted concrete block walls
(3) Steel walls

(4) Steel plate walls with energy-absorbing linings
(5) Barricades, such as those used for explosives operations, constructed of reinforced concrete, sand-filled/wood-sandwich walls, wood-lined steel plate, or earthen or rock berms
(6) Specifically engineered construction assemblies

7.3 Explosion Venting. When explosion venting is used, it shall be designed as follows:

(1) So that fragments will not strike other occupied buildings or emergency response staging areas
(2) So that fragments will not strike critical equipment (e.g., production, storage, utility services, and fire protection)
(3)*So that fragments will be intercepted by blast mats, energy-absorbing barrier walls, or earthen berms

7.4 Unauthorized Access. Properly posted doors, gates, fences, or other barriers shall be provided to prevent unauthorized access to the following:

(1) Laboratory work areas containing an explosion hazard
(2) Laboratory units containing an explosion hazard
(3) The space between explosion vents and fragment barriers

7.5 Inspection and Maintenance.

7.5.1 Inspection of all protective construction devices and systems shall be conducted at least annually.

7.5.2 Required maintenance shall be done to assure integrity and operability.

7.5.3* Explosion shields and special explosion-containing hoods shall be inspected prior to each use for deterioration, especially transparent shields and sight panels in special explosion-containing hoods.

Chapter 8 Laboratory Ventilating Systems and Hood Requirements

8.1* General.

8.1.1 This chapter shall apply to laboratory exhaust systems, including chemical fume hoods, special local exhaust devices, and other systems for exhausting air from laboratory work areas in which flammable gases, vapors, or particulate matter are released.

8.1.2 This chapter shall apply to laboratory air supply systems and shall provide requirements for identification, inspection, and maintenance of laboratory ventilation systems and hoods.

8.2 Basic Requirements.

8.2.1* Laboratory ventilation systems shall be designed to ensure that fire hazards and risks are minimized.

8.2.2* Laboratory units and laboratory hoods in which chemicals are present shall be continuously ventilated under normal operating conditions.

8.2.3* Chemical fume hoods shall not be relied upon to provide explosion (blast) protection unless specifically designed to do so. *(See also C.5.4 and C.5.5 for further information on explosion-resistant hoods and shields.)*

8.2.4 Chemical fume hoods using perchloric acid shall be in accordance with Section 8.11.

8.2.5 Exhaust and supply systems shall be designed to prevent a pressure differential that would impede egress or ingress when either system fails or during a fire or emergency scenario. This design includes reduced operational modes or shutdown of either the supply or the exhaust ventilation system.

8.2.6 The release of chemical vapors into the laboratory shall be controlled by enclosure(s) or captured to prevent any flammable and/or combustible concentrations of vapors from reaching any source of ignition.

8.3 Supply Systems.

8.3.1 Laboratory ventilation systems shall be designed to ensure that chemical fumes, vapors, or gases originating from the laboratory shall not be recirculated.

8.3.2* The location and configuration of fresh air intakes shall be chosen so as to avoid drawing in chemicals or products of combustion coming either from the laboratory building itself or from other structures and devices.

8.3.3 The air pressure in the laboratory work areas shall be negative with respect to corridors and non-laboratory areas of the laboratory unit except in the following instances:

(1) Where operations such as those requiring clean rooms preclude a negative pressure relative to surrounding areas, alternate means shall be provided to prevent escape of the atmosphere in the laboratory work area or unit to the surrounding spaces.
(2) The desired static pressure level with respect to corridors and non-laboratory areas shall be permitted to undergo momentary variations as the ventilation system components respond to door openings, changes in chemical fume hood sash positions, and other activities that can for a short term affect the static pressure level and its negative relationship.
(3) Laboratory work areas located within a designated electrically classified hazardous area with a positive air pressure system as described in NFPA 496, *Standard for Purged and Pressurized Enclosures for Electrical Equipment*, in accordance with Chapter 7, Pressurized Control Rooms shall be permitted to be positive with respect to adjacent corridors.

8.3.4* The location of air supply diffusion devices shall be chosen so as to avoid air currents that would adversely affect the performance of chemical fume hoods, exhaust systems, and fire detection or fire-extinguishing systems. *(See Sections 6.2, and 6.5, and 8.9.1.)*

8.4 Exhaust Air Discharge.

8.4.1* Air exhausted from chemical fume hoods and other special local exhaust systems shall not be recirculated. *(See also 8.3.1.)*

8.4.2* Energy Conservation Devices.

8.4.2.1 If energy conservation devices are used, they shall be designed in accordance with 8.3.1 and 8.3.2.

8.4.2.2 Devices that could result in recirculation of exhaust air or exhausted contaminants shall not be used unless designed in accordance with Section 4:10.1, "Nonlaboratory Air," and Section 4:10.2, "General Room Exhaust," of ANSI/AIHA Z9.5, *Laboratory Ventilation*.

8.4.3 Air exhausted from laboratory work areas shall not pass unducted through other areas.

8.4.4* Air from laboratory units and laboratory work areas in which chemicals are present shall be continuously discharged through duct systems maintained at a negative pressure relative to the pressure of normally occupied areas of the building.

8.4.5 Positive pressure portions of the lab hood exhaust systems (e.g., fans, coils, flexible connections, and ductwork) located within the laboratory building shall be sealed airtight or located in a continuously mechanically ventilated room.

8.4.6 Chemical fume hood face velocities and exhaust volumes shall be sufficient to contain contaminants generated within the hood and exhaust them outside of the laboratory building.

8.4.7* The hood shall provide containment of the possible hazards and protection for personnel at all times when chemicals are present in the hood.

8.4.8 Special local exhaust systems, such as snorkels or "elephant trunks," shall have sufficient capture velocities to entrain the chemical being released.

8.4.9* Canopy hoods shall not be used in lieu of chemical fume hoods.

8.4.10 Only Class II, Type B2 biological safety cabinets listed by the National Sanitation Foundation as meeting NSF/ANSI 49, *Class II (Laminar Flow) Biosafety Cabinetry*, shall be permitted to be used in lieu of chemical fume hoods, as determined by a qualified person.

8.4.11 Laminar flow cabinets shall not be used in lieu of chemical fume hoods.

8.4.12* Air exhausted from chemical fume hoods and special exhaust systems shall be discharged above the roof at a location, height, and velocity sufficient to prevent re-entry of chemicals and to prevent exposures to personnel.

8.5 Duct Construction for Hoods and Local Exhaust Systems.

8.5.1* Ducts from chemical fume hoods and from local exhaust systems shall be constructed entirely of noncombustible materials except in the following cases:

(1) Flexible ducts of combustible construction shall be permitted to be used for special local exhaust systems within a laboratory work area. *(See 8.5.2.)*
(2) Combustible ducts shall be permitted to be used if enclosed in a shaft of noncombustible or limited-combustible construction where they pass through non-laboratory areas or through laboratory units other than the one they serve. *(See 8.5.2.)*
(3) Combustible ducts shall be permitted to be used if all areas through which they pass are protected with an approved automatic fire-extinguishing system, as described in Chapter 6. *(See 8.5.2.)*

8.5.2 Combustible ducts or duct linings shall have a flame spread index of 25 or less when tested in accordance with ASTM E 84, *Standard Test Method for Surface Burning Characteristics of Building Materials*, or ANSI/UL 723, *Standard for Test for Surface Burning Characteristics of Building Materials*. Test specimens shall be of the minimum thickness used in the construction of the duct or duct lining.

8.5.3 Linings and coatings containing such fill as fiberglass, mineral wool, foam, or other similar material that could accumulate chemical deposits shall not be permitted within laboratory exhaust systems.

8.5.4 Duct systems for perchloric acid hoods shall be constructed in accordance with Section 8.11.

8.5.5 Ducts shall be of adequate strength and rigidity to meet the conditions of service and installation requirements and shall be protected against mechanical damage.

8.5.6 Materials used for vibration isolation connectors shall comply with 8.5.2.

8.5.7 Flexible connectors containing pockets in which conveyed material can collect shall not be used in any concealed space or where strong oxidizing chemicals (e.g., perchloric acid) are used.

8.5.8 Controls and dampers, where required for balancing or control of the exhaust system, shall be of a type that, in the event of failure, will fail open to ensure continuous draft. *(See 8.10.3 through 8.10.5.)*

8.5.9 Hand holes, where installed for damper, sprinkler, or fusible link inspection or resetting and for residue clean-out purposes, shall be equipped with tight-fitting covers provided with substantial fasteners.

8.5.10 Manifolding of Chemical Fume Hood and Ducts.

8.5.10.1 Exhaust ducts from each laboratory unit shall be separately ducted to a point outside the building, to a mechanical room, or to a shaft. *(See 5.1.5 and 8.10.3.)*

8.5.10.2 Connection to a common chemical fume hood exhaust duct system shall be permitted to occur within a building only in any of the following locations:

(1) Mechanical room protected in accordance with Table 5.1.1
(2) Shaft protected in accordance with the chapter for protection of vertical openings of NFPA *101, Life Safety Code*
(3) A point outside the building

8.5.10.3 Exhaust ducts from chemical fume hoods and other exhaust systems within the same laboratory unit shall be permitted to be combined within that laboratory unit. *(See 8.4.1.)*

8.6 Duct Velocities. Duct velocities of laboratory exhaust systems shall be high enough to minimize the deposition of liquids or condensable solids in the exhaust systems during normal operations in the chemical fume hood.

8.7 Exhausters (Fans), Controls, Velocities, and Discharge.

8.7.1 Fans shall be selected to meet requirements for fire, explosion, and corrosion.

8.7.2 Fans conveying both corrosive and flammable or combustible materials shall be permitted to be lined with or constructed of corrosion-resistant materials having a flame spread index of 25 or less when tested in accordance with ASTM E 84, *Standard Test Method for Surface Burning Characteristics of Building Materials*, or ANSI/UL 723, *Standard for Test for Surface Burning Characteristics of Building Materials*.

8.7.3 Fans shall be located and arranged so as to afford ready access for repairs, cleaning, inspection, and maintenance.

8.7.4* Where flammable gases, flammable vapors, or combustible dusts are passed through the fans, the rotating element shall be of nonferrous or spark-resistant construction; alternatively, the casing shall be constructed of or lined with such material.

8.7.4.1 Where there is the possibility of solid material passing through the fan that would produce a spark, both the rotating element and the casing shall be constructed of such material.

8.7.4.2 Nonferrous or spark-resistant materials shall have a flame spread index of 25 or less when tested in accordance with ASTM E 84, *Standard Test Method for Surface Burning Characteristics of Building Materials*, or ANSI/UL 723, *Standard for Test for Surface Burning Characteristics of Building Materials*.

8.7.5 Motors and their controls shall be located outside the location where flammable or combustible vapors or combustible dusts are generated or conveyed, unless specifically approved for that location and use.

8.7.6* Fans shall be marked with an arrow or other means to indicate direction of rotation and with the location of chemical fume hoods and exhaust systems served.

8.8 Chemical Fume Hood Construction. *(See also 8.2.2 and Section 8.11.)*

8.8.1 Chemical Fume Hood Interiors.

8.8.1.1* Materials of construction used for the interiors of new chemical fume hoods or for the modification of the interiors of existing chemical fume hoods shall have a flame spread index of 25 or less when tested in accordance with ASTM E 84, *Standard Test Method for Surface Burning Characteristics of Building Materials*, or ANSI/UL 723, *Standard for Test for Surface Burning Characteristics of Building Materials*, unless the interior of the hood is provided with automatic fire protection in accordance with 8.10.2.

8.8.1.2* Baffles shall be constructed so that they are unable to be adjusted to materially restrict the volume of air exhausted through the chemical fume hood.

8.8.1.3* Chemical fume hoods shall be provided with a means of preventing overflow of a spill of 2 L (0.5 gal) of liquid.

8.8.2* Chemical Fume Hood Sash Glazing. The sash, if provided, shall be glazed with material that will provide protection to the operator against the hazards associated with the use of the hood. *(See also Annex C.)*

8.8.3* Chemical Fume Hood Sash Closure.

8.8.3.1 Chemical fume hood sashes shall be kept closed whenever possible.

8.8.3.2 When a fume hood is unattended, its sash shall remain fully closed.

8.8.4* Electrical Devices.

8.8.4.1 In installations where services and controls are within the hood, additional electrical disconnects shall be located within 15 m (50 ft) of the hood and shall be accessible and clearly marked.

8.8.4.2 If electrical receptacles are located external to the hood, no additional electrical disconnect shall be required. *(See 5.6.1.)*

8.8.5 Other Hood Services.

8.8.5.1 For new installations or modifications of existing installations, controls for chemical fume hood services (gas, air, water, etc.) shall be located external to the hood and within easy reach.

8.8.5.2 In existing installations where service controls are within the hood, additional shutoffs shall be located within 15 m (50 ft) of the hood and shall be accessible and clearly marked.

8.8.6 Auxiliary Air. For auxiliary air hoods, auxiliary air shall be introduced exterior to the hood face in such a manner that the airflow does not compromise the protection provided by the hood and so that an imbalance of auxiliary air to exhaust air will not pressurize the hood interior.

8.8.7 Measuring Device for Hood Airflow. A measuring device for hood airflow shall be provided on each chemical fume hood.

8.8.7.1 The measuring device for hood airflow shall be a permanently installed device.

8.8.7.2 The measuring device for hood airflow shall provide constant indication to the hood user of adequate or inadequate hood airflow.

8.9 Chemical Fume Hood Location.

8.9.1* Chemical fume hoods shall be located in areas of minimum air turbulence.

8.9.2 Chemical fume hoods shall not be located adjacent to a single means of access to an exit or to high-traffic areas.

8.9.3* Work stations not directly related to the chemical fume hood activity shall not be located directly in front of chemical fume hood openings.

8.10 Chemical Fume Hood Fire Protection.

8.10.1* Automatic fire protection systems shall not be required in chemical fume hoods or exhaust systems except in the following cases:

(1) Existing hoods having interiors with a flame spread index greater than 25 in which flammable liquids are handled.
(2) If a hazard assessment shows that an automatic extinguishing system is required for the chemical fume hood, then the applicable automatic fire protection system standard shall be followed.

8.10.2 Automatic fire protection systems, where provided, shall comply with the following standards, as applicable:

(1) NFPA 11, *Standard for Low-, Medium-, and High-Expansion Foam*
(2) NFPA 12, *Standard on Carbon Dioxide Extinguishing Systems*
(3) NFPA 12A, *Standard on Halon 1301 Fire Extinguishing Systems*
(4) NFPA 13, *Standard for the Installation of Sprinkler Systems*
(5) NFPA 15, *Standard for Water Spray Fixed Systems for Fire Protection*
(6) NFPA 17, *Standard for Dry Chemical Extinguishing Systems*
(7) NFPA 17A, *Standard for Wet Chemical Extinguishing Systems*
(8) NFPA 69, *Standard on Explosion Prevention Systems*
(9) *NFPA 750, *Standard on Water Mist Fire Protection Systems*
(10) NFPA 2001, *Standard on Clean Agent Fire Extinguishing Systems*

8.10.2.1 The fire extinguishing system shall be suitable to extinguish fires within the chemical fume hood under the anticipated conditions of use.

8.10.3 The design and installation of ducts from chemical fume hoods shall be in accordance with NFPA 91, *Standard for Exhaust Systems for Air Conveying of Vapors, Gases, Mists, and Noncombustible Particulate Solids*, except that specific requirements in NFPA 45 shall take precedence.

8.10.3.1* Automatic fire dampers shall not be used in chemical fume hood exhaust systems.

8.10.4 Fire detection and alarm systems shall not be interlocked to automatically shut down chemical fume hood exhaust fans.

8.10.5 Proper door operation for egress shall be maintained when the supply system shuts down and the lab exhaust system operates, creating a pressure differential.

8.10.6 Chemical fume hoods equipped with control systems that vary the hood exhaust airflow as the sash opening varies and/or in conjunction with whether the laboratory room is in use (occupied or unoccupied) shall be equipped with a user-accessible means to attain maximum exhaust hood airflow regardless of sash position when necessary or desirable to ensure containment and removal of a potential hazard within the hood.

8.10.7* Chemical fume hoods shall be installed in a manner that prevents fire or smoke from a fire in the chemical fume hood from spreading into the voids above the ceiling.

8.11 Perchloric Acid Hoods.

8.11.1* Perchloric acid heated above ambient temperatures shall only be used in a chemical fume hood specifically designed for its use and identified as follows:

FOR PERCHLORIC ACID OPERATIONS

Exception: Hoods not specifically designed for use with perchloric acid shall be permitted to be used where the vapors are trapped and scrubbed before they are released into the hood. (See also 12.1.2.5.)

8.11.2 Perchloric acid hoods and exhaust ductwork shall be constructed of materials that are acid resistant, nonreactive, and impervious to perchloric acid.

8.11.3 The exhaust fan shall be acid resistant and spark resistant.

8.11.4 The exhaust fan motor shall not be located within the ductwork.

8.11.5 Drive belts shall be conductive and shall not be located within the ductwork.

8.11.6 Ductwork for perchloric acid hoods and exhaust systems shall take the shortest and straightest path to the outside of the building and shall not be manifolded with other exhaust systems.

8.11.6.1 Horizontal runs shall be as short as possible, with no sharp turns or bends.

8.11.6.2 The ductwork shall provide a positive drainage slope back into the hood.

8.11.6.3 Ductwork shall consist of sealed sections.

8.11.6.4 Flexible connectors shall not be used.

8.11.7 Sealants, gaskets, and lubricants used with perchloric acid hoods, ductwork, and exhaust systems shall be acid resistant and nonreactive with perchloric acid.

8.11.8* A water spray system shall be provided for washing down the hood interior behind the baffle and the entire exhaust system.

8.11.8.1 The hood work surface shall be watertight with a minimum depression of 13 mm (½ in.) at the front and sides.

8.11.8.2 An integral trough shall be provided at the rear of the hood to collect washdown water.

8.11.9 The hood baffle shall be removable for inspection and cleaning.

8.11.10* If a chemical fume hood or exhaust system was used for perchloric acid heated above ambient temperature, tests shall be conducted for explosive perchlorates before any inspection, cleaning, maintenance, or any other work is done on any part of the exhaust system or hood interior.

8.11.11 Prior to using a perchloric acid hood for any purpose, the hood shall be water-washed and shall be tested according to 8.11.9 to ensure residual perchlorates are not present.

8.12 Identification of Chemical Fume Hood Systems.

8.12.1* Special-use chemical fume hoods and special-use local exhaust systems shall be identified to indicate their intended use.

8.12.2 A sign containing the following information from the last inspection shall be affixed to each hood, or a properly maintained log of all hoods providing the following information shall be maintained:

(1) Inspection interval
(2) Last inspection date
(3) Average face velocity
(4) Location of fan that serves hood
(5) Inspector's name

8.13 Inspection, Testing, and Maintenance.

8.13.1* When installed or modified and at least annually thereafter, chemical fume hoods, chemical fume hood exhaust systems, and laboratory special exhaust systems shall be inspected and tested as applicable, as follows:

(1) Visual inspection of the physical condition of the hood interior, sash, and ductwork *(see 7.5.3)*
(2) Measuring device for hood airflow
(3) Low airflow and loss-of-airflow alarms at each alarm location
(4) Face velocity
(5) Verification of inward airflow over the entire hood face
(6) Changes in work area conditions that might affect hood performance

8.13.2 Deficiencies in hood performance shall be corrected, or one of the following shall apply:

(1) The activity within the hood shall be restricted to the capability of the hood.
(2) The hood shall not be used.

8.13.3 Chemical fume hood face velocity profile or hood exhaust air quantity shall be checked after any adjustment to the ventilation system balance.

8.13.4 Detectors and Alarms.

8.13.4.1 Air system flow detectors, if installed, shall be inspected and tested annually.

8.13.4.2 Where potentially corrosive or obstructive conditions exist, the inspection and test frequency shall be increased.

8.13.5 Fans and Motors.

8.13.5.1* Air supply and exhaust fans, motors, and components shall be inspected at least annually.

8.13.5.2 Where airflow detectors are not provided or airflow-rate tests are not made, fan belts shall be inspected quarterly; double sheaves and belts shall be permitted to be inspected semiannually.

8.13.5.3 Frayed or broken belts shall be replaced promptly.

8.13.6 Fixed fire-extinguishing systems protecting filters shall be inspected quarterly for accumulation of deposits on nozzles and cleaned as necessary.

Chapter 9 Chemical Storage, Handling, and Waste Disposal

9.1* Ordering Procedures.

9.1.1 When a chemical is ordered, steps shall be taken to determine its hazards and to transmit that information to those who will receive, store, use, or dispose of the chemical.

9.1.2 Restrictions imposed by governmental regulations and in-house rules shall be followed.

9.2 Handling and Storage.

9.2.1 Facilities.

9.2.1.1 Chemicals shall not be brought into a laboratory work area unless the design, construction, and fire protection of receiving and storage facilities are commensurate with the quantities and hazards of chemicals involved.

9.2.1.2 Safe storage facilities shall be provided for materials that have unique physical or hazardous properties, such as temperature sensitivity, water reactivity, or explosibility. *(See A.9.1 for sources of additional information.)*

9.2.1.3 Hazardous chemicals shall be stored and handled in such a manner as to limit a spill scenario to less than 20 L (5 gal).

9.2.2 Handling.

9.2.2.1* Receiving, transporting, unpacking, and dispensing of chemicals and other hazardous materials shall be carried out by trained personnel in such locations and in such a manner as to minimize hazards from flammable, reactive, or toxic materials.

9.2.2.2* Materials of construction for ducts, piping, and vessels shall be compatible with materials to be transferred or handled.

9.2.2.3 Before a chemical material is used, the user shall determine that information and facilities are available for safe disposal of hazardous materials and waste products.

9.2.2.4 Class I liquids shall not be transferred from one vessel to another in any exit access corridor.

9.2.2.5 Pressurized liquid dispensing containers containing chemicals shall be in accordance with Section 10.4.

9.2.2.6 Chemical quantities outside of storage shall be maintained at the lowest possible level necessary for the work performed.

9.2.2.7 Handling and storage of chemicals shall conform to the manufacturers' recommendations and material safety data sheet (MSDS).

9.2.3 Storage.

9.2.3.1* Chemical inventories in each laboratory unit shall be maintained within the maximum allowable quantities specified in the applicable fire prevention code or building code except as modified in Chapter 10 for buildings with more than three stories.

9.2.3.1.1 Maximum allowable quantities shall be reduced by 50 percent for Class B laboratory units located above the third floor.

9.2.3.1.2 Maximum allowable quantities shall be reduced by 25 percent for Class C and Class D laboratory units located on the fourth through sixth floors of a building.

9.2.3.1.3 Maximum allowable quantities shall be reduced by 50 percent for Class C and Class D laboratory units located above the sixth floor.

9.2.3.2* Incompatible materials shall be segregated to prevent accidental contact with one another.

9.2.3.3 Class I flammable liquids and Class II combustible liquids that are not in use inside of laboratory units shall be stored in safety cans; in approved storage cabinets constructed in accordance with NFPA 30, *Flammable and Combustible Liquids Code*, and ANSI/UL 1275, *Standard for Flammable Liquid Cabinets*; or in an inside liquid storage area.

9.2.3.4* Containers of materials that might become hazardous (i.e., time sensitive) during prolonged storage shall be dated when first opened, and properly managed.

9.2.3.4.1* Proper management shall consist of the following elements:

(1) Defining those materials present that are time sensitive
(2) Defining each time-sensitive material's inspection frequency
(3) Defining proper or approved inspection methodologies to determine the relative hazard of the time-sensitive material
(4) Defining pass/fail criteria for inspection results

9.2.3.4.2 Time-sensitive materials that pass inspection shall be permitted to be redated and retained for an additional defined inspection period.

9.2.3.4.3 All other material shall be safely discarded.

9.2.3.5* Storage cabinets used in laboratories shall not be required to be vented for fire protection purposes.

9.2.3.6 Laboratory storage facilities shall be inspected to ensure compliance with the provisions of Chapter 9.

9.2.3.7 Storage of chemicals in the fume hood shall be prohibited.

9.3 Waste Handling and Disposal.

9.3.1 Waste chemicals shall be handled and stored according to the requirements in Section 9.2.

9.3.2 Waste chemicals shall not be combined or mixed with other waste chemicals unless they have been evaluated for compatibility by a qualified person.

9.3.3 Chemical waste containers shall be labeled with the hazards of the waste chemicals.

9.3.4 Liquid waste containers stored in laboratory work areas shall not exceed 20 L (5 gal).

9.3.5 Waste quantities shall be subject to the maximum container sizes and type in accordance with Table 10.1.2.

9.3.6 Waste quantities shall be subject to the maximum allowable quantity for the laboratory unit.

Chapter 10 Flammable and Combustible Liquids

10.1 Quantity Limitations.

10.1.1 The density and total amount of flammable and combustible liquids in use in laboratory work areas and in the laboratory unit outside of flammable liquid storage rooms shall not exceed the quantities presented in Table 10.1.1(a) and Table 10.1.1(b) for the respective class of laboratory.

10.1.2* Container types and maximum capacities for flammable and combustible liquids shall comply with Table 10.1.2 except as follows:

(1) Glass containers as large as 4 L (1 gal) shall be permitted to be used if all the following conditions are present:
   (a) Excessive corrosion or degradation of a metal or an approved plastic container would result.
   (b) The glass container size allowed in Table 10.1.2 is not available.
   (c) The glass containers are required for purity purposes.
(2) Containers of not more than 227 L (60 gal) capacity shall be permitted in a separate area inside the building if the inside area meets the requirements of NFPA 30, *Flammable and Combustible Liquids Code.*
(3) In educational and instructional laboratory work areas, containers for Class I or Class II liquids shall not exceed the following capacity:
   (a) Safety cans of 8 L (2.1 gal)
   (b) Other containers of 4 L (1 gal)

10.2 Supply Piping.
Supply piping for flammable and combustible liquid supply systems shall comply with NFPA 30, *Flammable and Combustible Liquids Code.*

10.3 Liquid Dispensing.

10.3.1* Dispensing of Class I liquids to or from containers less than or equal to 20 L (5 gal) in capacity shall be performed in one of the following locations:

(1) In a chemical fume hood
(2) In an area provided with ventilation adequate to prevent accumulations of flammable vapor/air mixtures from exceeding 25 percent of the lower flammable limit
(3) Inside liquid storage areas specifically designed and protected for dispensing Class I flammable liquids that meet the requirements of NFPA 30, *Flammable and Combustible Liquids Code*

10.3.2* Except for pressurized liquid dispensing containers meeting the requirements of Section 10.4, dispensing of Class I liquids to or from containers greater than 20 L (5 gal) shall be performed in one of the following locations:

(1) In a separate area outside the building
(2) Inside liquid storage areas specifically designed and protected for dispensing Class I flammable liquids that meet the requirements of NFPA 30, *Flammable and Combustible Liquids Code*

10.3.3* Class I liquids shall not be transferred between conductive containers of greater than 4 L (1 gal) capacity unless the containers are electrically interconnected by direct bonding or by indirect bonding through a common grounding system.

10.3.4 When dispensing Class I liquids involves nonconductive containers larger than 4 L (1 gal), which can be difficult to bond or ground, special dispensing procedures commensu-

Table 10.1.1(a) Maximum Quantities of Flammable and Combustible Liquids in Laboratory Units Outside of Inside Liquid Storage Areas (Metric)

Laboratory Unit Fire Hazard Class	Flammable and Combustible Liquid Class[a]	Quantities in Use[a]		Quantities in Use and Storage[a]	
		Maximum Quantity[b] per 9.3 m^2 of Laboratory Unit[c]	Maximum Quantity[b] per Laboratory Unit	Maximum Quantity[b] per 9.3 m^2 of Laboratory Unit[c]	Maximum Quantity[b] per Laboratory Unit
		L	L	L	L
A (high fire hazard)	I	38	1820	76	1820
	I, II, and IIIA	76	3028	150	6060
B[d] (moderate fire hazard)	I	20	1136	38	1820
	I, II, and IIIA	38	1515	76	3028
C[e] (low fire hazard)	I	7.5	570	15	1136
	I, II, and IIIA	15	757	30	1515
D[e] (minimal fire hazard)	I	4	284	7.5	570
	I, II, and IIIA	4	284	7.5	570

Note: For maximum container sizes, see Table 10.1.2.

[a]The maximum amount in use in open systems is limited to 10 percent of the quantities listed.

[b]See 4.2.2 for additional requirements for educational and instructional laboratories.

[c]The quantities per 9.3 m^2 do not imply the quantities must be within that 9.3 m^2 area; the quantities per 9.3 m^2 are for calculation purposes to determine the total quantity allowed per laboratory work area and the total amount overall in the laboratory unit.

[d]Reduce quantities by 50 percent for B laboratory units located above the 3rd floor.

[e]Reduce quantities by 25 percent for C and D laboratory units located on the 4th–6th floors of a building and reduce quantities by 50 percent for C and D laboratory units located above the 6th floor.

rate with the electrical characteristics of the liquid shall be developed and implemented.

10.4 Pressurized Liquid Dispensing Containers (PLDC).

10.4.1 Pressurized liquid dispensing containers used for flammable and combustible liquids shall be listed or labeled for their intended use by a nationally recognized testing laboratory.

10.4.2 Nonmetallic containers larger than 4 L (1 gal) shall not be used.

10.4.3* Relief devices shall discharge to a safe location, in accordance with the manufacturer's recommendation.

10.4.4 The piping/hose between the container and the use point shall be rated for the pressure, compatible with the materials being transferred, and not subject to mechanical damage.

10.4.5 Prior to pressurizing the system, all fittings and connections shall be secure and leak free.

10.4.6* A readily accessible means to stop the flow of liquid from the container shall be provided.

10.4.7 Containers shall be pressurized only with nitrogen or inert gas; air shall not be used.

10.4.8 A means to prevent backflow into the gas supply system shall be provided.

10.5 Equipment.

10.5.1 Storage cabinets used for the storage of flammable and combustible liquids shall be constructed in accordance with NFPA 30, *Flammable and Combustible Liquids Code*.

10.5.2 Flammable liquids stored in refrigerated equipment shall be stored in closed containers. *(See 12.2.2.)*

10.5.3* Laboratory heating equipment such as ovens, furnaces, environmental chambers, and other heated enclosures shall not be used to heat, store, or test flammable or combustible liquids or aerosols containing flammable gases unless the equipment is designed or modified to prevent internal explosion.

10.5.4 Baths handling flammable liquids or combustible liquids heated to their flash points shall be placed in a chemical fume hood or shall be vented to a safe location to control vapors.

10.5.5 Electric motors shall be suitable for Class I, Division 2 locations when flammable and combustible liquids or flammable gas concentrations can produce hazardous concentrations of flammable mixtures.

Exception: Electric motors shall be exempt from this requirement if they are located in chemical fume hoods or provided with special local ventilation that will prevent flammable concentrations of gases or vapors from reaching the motor.

Table 10.1.1(b) Maximum Quantities of Flammable and Combustible Liquids in Laboratory Units Outside of Inside Liquid Storage Areas (U.S. Customary Units)

Laboratory Unit Fire Hazard Class	Flammable and Combustible Liquid Class[a]	Quantities in Use[a]		Quantities in Use and Storage[a]	
		Maximum Quantity[b] per 100 ft² of Laboratory Unit[c]	Maximum Quantity[b] per Laboratory Unit	Maximum Quantity[b] per 100 ft² of Laboratory Unit[c]	Maximum Quantity[b] per Laboratory Unit
		gal	gal	gal	gal
A (high fire hazard)	I	10	480	20	480
	I, II, and IIIA	20	800	40	1600
B[d] (moderate fire hazard)	I	5	300	10	480
	I, II, and IIIA	10	400	20	800
C[e] (low fire hazard)	I	2	150	4	300
	I, II, and IIIA	4	200	8	400
D[e] (minimal fire hazard)	I	1	75	2	150
	I, II, and IIIA	1	75	2	150

Note: For maximum container sizes, see Table 10.1.2.

[a]The maximum amount in use in open systems is limited to 10 percent of the quantities listed.

[b]See 4.2.2 for additional requirements for educational and instructional laboratories.

[c]The quantities per 100 ft² do not imply the quantities must be within that 100 ft² area; the quantities per 100 ft² are for calculation purposes to determine the total quantity allowed per laboratory work area and the total amount overall in the laboratory unit.

[d] Reduce quantities by 50 percent for B laboratory units located above the 3rd floor.

[e] Reduce quantities by 25 percent for C and D laboratory units located on the 4th–6th floors of a building and reduce quantities by 50 percent for C and D laboratory units located above the 6th floor.

Table 10.1.2 Maximum Allowable Container Capacity

Container Type	Flammable Liquids[a]			Combustible Liquids[a]	
	IA	IB	IC	II	IIIA
Glass	500 mL (1 pt)[b]	1 L (1 qt)[b]	4 L (1 gal)	4 L (1 gal)	20 L (5 gal)
Metal (other than DOT drums) or approved plastic	4 L (1 gal)	20 L (5 gal)[c]	20 L (5 gal)[c]	20 L (5 gal)[c]	20 L (5 gal)
Safety cans	10 L (2.6 gal)[c]	20 L (5 gal)[c]	20 L (5 gal)[c]	20 L (5 gal)[c]	20 L (5 gal)
Metal container (DOT specification)	4 L (1 gal)	20 L (5 gal)[c]	20 L (5 gal)[c]	227 L (60 gal)[c]	227 L (60 gal)
Polyethylene (DOT Specification 34, UN 1H1, or as authorized by DOT special permit)	4 L (1 gal)	20 L (5 gal)[c]	20 L (5 gal)[c]	227 L (60 gal)[c]	227 L (60 gal)
Pressurized liquid dispensing container	20 L (5 gal)	227 L (60 gal)	227 L (60 gal)	227 L (60 gal)	227 L (60 gal)

Note: This table is based on Table 6.2.3 of NFPA 30, *Flammable and Combustible Liquids Code*, except for allowable quantities of flammable liquids in metal (DOT specification) drums and pressurized liquid dispensing containers.

[a]See B.1 for definitions of the various classes of flammable and combustible liquids.

[b]See 10.1.2(1) and A.10.1.2.

[c]See 10.1.2(3).

Chapter 11 Compressed and Liquefied Gases

11.1 Compressed and Liquefied Gases in Cylinders.

11.1.1 Cylinders shall be handled only by trained personnel. *(See Annex E and Annex F.)*

11.1.2* Cylinders, except nominal 0.5 kg (1 lb) propane cylinders made for consumer use, that are not necessary for current laboratory requirements shall be stored outside the laboratory unit in accordance with NFPA 55, *Compressed Gases and Cryogenic Fluids Code*.

11.1.3* Any compressed gas cylinder or container used at gauge pressures over 103 kPa (15 psi) shall be fabricated to the specifications of or authorized for use by the U.S. DOT, T.C., or Section VIII of the ASME *Boiler and Pressure Vessel Code*.

11.1.3.1 The container shall be marked to show the authorizing code and its working pressure at 21°C (70°F).

11.1.3.2 Vessels whose physical size, operating pressure, or both, are outside the scope of the referenced code(s) shall be constructed in accordance with the philosophy and guidance of the ASME *Boiler and Pressure Vessel Code* and shall not require marking.

11.1.4 Special Ventilation Requirements for Gas Cylinders.

11.1.4.1 This section shall not apply to gases that have a health rating of 3, as rated in NFPA 704, *Standard System for the Identification of the Hazards of Materials for Emergency Response*, if they are rated as such by virtue of it being a cryogenic, with no other health hazards.

11.1.4.2 Lecture bottle–sized cylinders of the following gases located in laboratory units shall be kept in a continuously mechanically ventilated hood or other continuously mechanically ventilated enclosure:

(1) All gases that have health hazard ratings of 3 or 4
(2) All gases that have a health hazard rating of 2 without physiological warning properties
(3) Pyrophoric gases

11.1.4.3 Cylinders of all gases that are greater than lecture bottle size and have health hazard ratings of 3 or 4 and cylinders of gases that have a health hazard rating of 2 without physiological warning properties that are located in laboratory units shall meet both the following conditions:

(1) Storage in approved continuously mechanically ventilated gas cabinets
(2) Compliance with NFPA 55, *Compressed Gases and Cryogenic Fluids Code*

11.1.4.4 Cylinders of pyrophoric gases that are greater than lecture bottle size that are located in laboratory units shall be kept in approved continuously mechanically ventilated, sprinklered gas cabinets.

11.1.5 Cylinder Safety.

11.1.5.1 Cylinders shall be secured from tipping over by holders designed for such service.

11.1.5.2 Cylinders in the laboratory shall be equipped with a pressure regulator designed for the specific gas and marked for its maximum cylinder pressure.

11.1.5.2.1 The regulator system shall be equipped with two gauges, either on the regulator or remote from the regulator, installed so as to show both the cylinder pressure and the outlet pressure.

11.1.5.2.2 Where the source cylinder is outside of the laboratory, a station regulator and gauge shall be installed at the point of use to show outlet pressure.

11.1.5.3 Cylinders shall have a manual shutoff valve. A quick connect shall not be used in place of a shutoff valve.

11.1.6 Cylinders in Use.

11.1.6.1 Cylinders, when in use, shall be connected to gas delivery systems designed by a qualified person.

11.1.6.2 Cylinders shall be attached to an instrument for use by means of a regulator.

11.1.6.3 A compressed gas cylinder shall be considered to be "in use" if it is in compliance with one of the following:

(1) Connected through a regulator to deliver gas to a laboratory operation
(2) Connected to a manifold being used to deliver gas to a laboratory operation
(3) A single cylinder secured alongside the cylinder described in 11.1.6.3(1) as the reserve cylinder for the cylinder described in 11.1.6.3(1)

11.1.6.4 Cylinders not "in use" shall not be stored in the laboratory unit.

11.1.6.5 The quantity of compressed and liquefied gases in Class A, Class B, and Class C laboratory units shall be in accordance with the amounts listed in Table 6.3.1 of NFPA 55, *Compressed Gases and Cryogenic Fluids Code*.

11.1.6.6 The number of lecture bottle cylinders in Class A, Class B, and Class C laboratory units shall be limited to 25.

11.1.6.7 The quantity of compressed and liquefied gases in Class D laboratory units shall be limited to 50 percent of the amounts listed in Table 6.3.1 of NFPA 55, *Compressed Gases and Cryogenic Fluids Code*,

11.1.6.8 In instructional laboratory work areas, the quantity of compressed and liquefied gases shall be limited to 10 percent of the amounts listed in Table 6.3.1 of NFPA 55, *Compressed Gases and Cryogenic Fluids Code*, or 10 lecture bottle–sized cylinders.

11.1.6.9 In educational laboratory work areas, the quantity of compressed and liquefied gases shall be limited as follows:

(1) The maximum quantity of flammable gas shall not exceed 2.8 m³ (100 ft³).
(2) The maximum quantity of oxidizing gas shall not exceed 2.8 m³ (100 ft³).
(3) A maximum of two 0.5 kg (1 lb) liquefied flammable gas cylinders shall be permitted.
(4) Health hazard 3 and 4 gases shall not be permitted

11.2 Storage and Piping Systems.

11.2.1* The method of storage and piping systems for compressed and liquefied gases shall comply with the applicable requirements of NFPA standards, including the following:

(1) NFPA 51, *Standard for the Design and Installation of Oxygen–Fuel Gas Systems for Welding, Cutting, and Allied Processes*
(2) NFPA 54, *National Fuel Gas Code*
(3) NFPA 55, *Compressed Gases and Cryogenic Fluids Code*
(4) NFPA 58, *Liquefied Petroleum Gas Code*

11.2.2 Systems for other compressed gases and for cryogenic materials shall comply with the manufacturer's design and specifications.

11.2.3* Each point of use shall have an accessible manual shutoff valve.

11.2.3.1 The manual shutoff valve at the point of use shall be located away from the potential hazards and be located within 1.8 m (6 ft) of the point of use.

11.2.3.2 Where the cylinder valve is located within immediate reach, a separate point-of-use shutoff valve shall not be required.

11.2.3.3 Line regulators that have their source away from the point of use shall have a manual shutoff valve.

11.2.3.4 An emergency gas shutoff device in an accessible location at the exit shall be provided in addition to the manual point-of-use valve in each educational and instructional laboratory space that has a piped gas–dispensing valve.

11.2.4 Each and every portion of a piping system shall have uninterruptible pressure relief.

11.2.4.1 Any part of the system that can be isolated from the rest of the system shall have adequate pressure relief.

11.2.4.2 Piping shall be designed for a pressure greater than the maximum system pressure that can be developed under abnormal conditions.

11.2.4.3 A pressure relief system shall be designed to provide a discharge rate sufficient to avoid further pressure increase and shall vent to a safe location.

11.2.5* Permanent piping shall be identified at the supply point and at each discharge point with the name of the material being transported.

11.2.6* Piping systems, including regulators, shall not be used for gases other than those for which they are designed and identified unless a thorough review of the design specifications, materials of construction, and service compatibility is made and other appropriate modifications have been made.

11.3 Outdoor Installation of Compressed Gas Cylinders for Servicing Laboratory Work Areas (Located Outside of Laboratory Work Areas).

11.3.1 Compressed gas cylinders installed or stored outside of laboratory buildings shall be installed and operated in accordance with the requirements in NFPA 55, *Compressed Gases and Cryogenic Fluids Code.*

11.3.2 Compressed gas delivery systems shall be designed in accordance with NFPA 55, *Compressed Gases and Cryogenic Fluids Code.*

11.4 Cryogenic Fluids.

11.4.1 All system components used for cryogenic fluids shall be selected and designed for such service.

11.4.1.1 Design pressure for vessels and piping shall be not less than 150 percent of maximum pressure relief.

11.4.1.2* Systems or apparatus handling a cryogenic fluid that can cause freezing or liquefaction of the surrounding atmosphere shall be designed to prevent contact of the condensed air with organic materials.

11.4.1.3 Systems or apparatus handling liquid oxygen shall be designed to prevent contact of the oxygen with organic materials.

11.4.2 Pressure relief of vessels and piping handling cryogenic fluids shall comply with the applicable requirements of Section 11.2.

11.4.3 The space in which cryogenic systems are located shall be ventilated commensurate with the properties of the specific cryogenic fluid in use.

Chapter 12 Laboratory Operations and Apparatus

12.1 Operations.

12.1.1* Hazards of Chemicals and Chemical Reactions. Experiments and tests conducted in educational and instructional laboratory units shall be under the direct supervision of an instructor.

12.1.1.1 Before laboratory tests or chemical reactions are begun, evaluations shall be made for hazards that can be encountered or generated during the course of the work.

12.1.1.2 Evaluations shall include the hazards associated with the properties and the reactivity of the materials used and any intermediate and end products that can be formed, hazards associated with the operation of the equipment at the operating conditions, and hazards associated with the proposed reactions — for example, oxidation and polymerization. *(See also 12.1.1.4.)*

12.1.1.3 Regular reviews of laboratory operations and procedures shall be conducted with special attention given to any change in materials, operations, or personnel.

12.1.1.4* Where reactions are being performed to synthesize materials, the hazard characteristics of which have not yet been determined by test, precautions shall be employed to control the highest possible hazard based on a known hazard of similar material.

12.1.1.5 Where use of a new material might present a severe explosion potential, initial experiments or tests shall be conducted in an enclosure that is designed to protect people and property from potential explosion damage. *(See Chapter 7.)*

12.1.1.6 Unattended or automatic laboratory operations involving hazardous chemicals shall be provided with regular surveillance for abnormal conditions. *(See 12.1.2.4 and 12.2.4.1.)*

12.1.2 Heating Operations.

12.1.2.1 All heating of flammable or combustible liquids shall be conducted so as to minimize fire hazards.

12.1.2.2 Provisions shall be made to contain liquid that might be accidentally released from glass apparatus containing more than 0.25 L (8.4 oz) of flammable liquid or combustible liquid heated to its flash point.

12.1.2.3 Supplementary fire-extinguishing equipment shall be provided, if necessary.

12.1.2.4 Unattended operations shall be provided with override control and automatic shutdown to prevent system failure that can result in fire or explosion.

12.1.2.5 Strong oxidizing materials, such as perchloric acid, shall not be heated by gas flames or oil baths.

12.1.3 Distillation Operations.

12.1.3.1 Distillations shall be conducted in equipment designed and fabricated for this use and shall be assembled with consideration being given to fire hazards from vent gases and possible equipment breakage or failure.

12.1.3.2 Care shall be taken to avoid the presence of unstable components (e.g., peroxides) in the still pot and to avoid overheating still contents.

12.1.3.3 Glass equipment used for distillations shall be inspected for cracks, scratches, and other defects prior to each use.

12.1.3.4 Faulty glass equipment shall be discarded or repaired.

12.1.4* Other Separation Operations. Filtrations, extractions, sublimations, adsorptions, evaporations, centrifuging operations, and other separation techniques that involve flammable or combustible materials shall be protected from ignition sources and shall be provided with ventilation that prevents the accumulation of an ignitible concentration of vapors in the work area.

12.1.5 Mixing and Grinding Operations.

12.1.5.1 Mixing, grinding, stirring, and agitating operations involving flammable and combustible materials shall require the same precautions against fire as set forth in 12.1.4.

12.1.5.2 Precautions shall be taken to avoid local overheating during grinding and mixing of solids.

12.1.5.3 Care shall be taken to avoid fire or explosion hazards from flammable or combustible materials.

12.1.6 Other Operations.

12.1.6.1 Other laboratory operations, such as reactions at temperatures and pressures either above or below ambient conditions, shall be conducted in a manner that minimizes hazards.

12.1.6.2 Shielding shall be used whenever there is a reasonable probability of explosion or vigorous chemical reaction and associated hazards during charging, sampling, venting, and discharge of products. *(See Chapter 7 and 12.2.5.)*

12.1.6.3 Glass apparatus containing gas or vapors under vacuum or above ambient pressure shall be shielded, wrapped with tape, or otherwise protected from shattering (such as engineering controls or by apparatus design) during use.

12.1.6.4* Quantities of reactants shall be limited and procedures shall be developed to control or isolate vigorous or exothermic reactions.

12.1.6.5 Flammable gases or vapors evolved during drying operations shall be condensed, trapped, or vented to avoid ignition.

12.1.6.6 Spraying of flammable or combustible paint and varnishes shall comply with the requirements of NFPA 33, *Standard for Spray Application Using Flammable or Combustible Materials.*

12.2 Apparatus.

12.2.1 General.

12.2.1.1 Apparatus shall be installed in compliance with applicable requirements of NFPA standards, including *NFPA 70, National Electrical Code.*

12.2.1.2 Operating controls shall be accessible under normal and emergency conditions.

12.2.2 Refrigeration and Cooling Equipment.

12.2.2.1* Each refrigerator, freezer, or cooler shall be prominently marked to indicate whether it meets the requirements for safe storage of flammable liquids.

12.2.2.2* Refrigerators, freezers, and other cooling equipment used to store or cool flammable liquids shall be listed as special purpose units for use in laboratories or equipment listed for Class I, Division 1 locations, as described in Article 501 of *NFPA 70, National Electrical Code.*

12.2.2.2.1* Domestic refrigerators, freezers, and other cooling equipment shall be permitted to store or cool flammable liquids if modified as follows:

(1) Any electrical equipment located within the outer shell, within the storage compartment, on the door, or on the door frame shall meet the requirements for Class I, Division 1 locations, as described in Article 501 of *NFPA 70, National Electrical Code.*
(2) Electrical equipment mounted on the outside of the storage compartment shall be installed in one of the following ways:
   (a) To meet the requirements for Class I, Division 2 locations
   (b) To be located above the storage compartment
   (c) To be located on the outside surface of the equipment where exposure to hazardous concentrations of vapors will be minimal

12.2.2.3 Refrigerators, freezers, and cooling equipment located in a laboratory work area designated as a Class I location, as specified in the Exception to 5.6.2, shall be approved for Class I, Division 1 or 2 locations and shall be installed in accordance with Article 501 of *NFPA 70, National Electrical Code.*

12.2.3 Heating Equipment.

12.2.3.1 All unattended electrical heating equipment shall be equipped with a manual reset over-temperature shutoff switch, in addition to normal temperature controls, if overheating could result in a fire or explosion.

12.2.3.2 Heating equipment with circulation fans or water cooling shall be equipped with an interlock arranged to disconnect current to the heating elements if the fan fails or the water supply is interrupted.

12.2.3.3 Burners, induction heaters, ovens, furnaces, and other heat-producing equipment shall be located a safe distance from areas where temperature-sensitive and flammable materials and compressed gases are handled.

12.2.3.4 Oven and furnace installations shall comply with NFPA 86, *Standard for Ovens and Furnaces.*

12.2.4 Heated Constant Temperature Baths.

12.2.4.1 Electrically heated constant temperature baths shall be equipped with over-temperature shutoff switches in addition to normal temperature controls, if overheating could result in a fire or an explosion.

12.2.4.2 Bath containers shall be of noncombustible materials.

12.2.5 Pressure Equipment.

12.2.5.1* Equipment used at pressures above 103 kPa gauge (15 psi) shall be designed and constructed by qualified individuals for use at the expected temperature, pressure, and other operating conditions affecting safety.

12.2.5.2 Pressure equipment shall be fitted with a pressure relief device, such as a rupture disc or a relief valve. The pressure relief device shall be vented to a safe location.

12.2.5.3 Equipment operated at pressures above 103 kPa gauge (15 psi), such as autoclaves, steam sterilizers, reactors, and calorimeters, shall be operated and maintained according to manufacturers' instructions, the design limitations of the equipment, and applicable codes and regulations.

12.2.5.3.1 Such equipment shall be inspected on a regular basis.

12.2.5.3.2 Any significant change in the condition of the equipment, such as corrosion, cracks, distortion, scale formation, or general chemical attack, or any weakening of the closure, or any inability of the equipment to maintain pressure, shall be documented and removed from service immediately and shall not be returned to service until approved by a qualified person.

12.2.5.4 Any pressure equipment that has been found to be degraded shall be derated or discarded, whichever is appropriate.

12.2.6 Analytical Instruments.

12.2.6.1 Analytical instruments, such as infrared, ultraviolet, atomic absorption, x-ray, mass spectrometers, chromatographs, and thermal analyzers, shall be installed in accordance with the manufacturers' instructions and applicable standards and codes.

12.2.6.2 Analytical instruments shall be operated in accordance with manufacturers' instructions or approved recommended operating procedures.

12.2.6.3 Hazards to personnel from high voltage, vapors or fumes, radiation, flames, flashbacks, and explosions shall be minimized.

Chapter 13   Hazard Identification

13.1 Identification of Entrances.

13.1.1* Entrances to laboratory units, laboratory work areas, storage areas, and associated facilities shall be identified by signs to warn emergency response personnel of unusual or severe hazards that are not directly related to the fire hazard of contents.

13.1.2 The hazards shall be communicated in the plans for fire fighting. *(See 6.6.3.1.)*

13.2* Exhaust Systems. Exhaust systems used for the removal of hazardous materials shall be identified to warn personnel of the possible hazards.

13.3 Labeling of Containers.

13.3.1 Content identification, including precautionary information, shall be provided directly on all original and subsequent containers of hazardous chemicals, except those being used in ongoing experiments.

13.3.2 Containers of materials that become hazardous during prolonged storage shall be dated when first opened, to facilitate hazard control. *(See 9.2.3.4 and A.9.2.3.4.)*

13.4 Identification Systems. Graphic systems used to identify hazards shall comply with ANSI Z535.1, *Safety Color Code*; ANSI Z535.2, *Environmental and Facility Safety Signs*; ANSI Z535.3, *Criteria for Safety Symbols*; and ANSI Z535.4, *Product Safety Signs and Labels*; or other approved graphic systems.

Annex A   Explanatory Material

Annex A is not a part of the requirements of this NFPA document but is included for informational purposes only. This annex contains explanatory material, numbered to correspond with the applicable text paragraphs.

A.1.1.2(1) Either condition of 1.1.2(1) meeting the minimum quantity will bring the lab within the scope of NFPA 45. A school lab with a low pressure natural gas system supplying Bunsen burners (with less than the minimum quantities of combustible or flammable liquids and less than the minimum quantities of other flammable gases) is an example of a lab outside the scope of NFPA 45.

A.1.1.2(2) The hazards of pilot plants are primarily based on the process, the chemistry, and the equipment, not the laboratory environment.

A.1.1.2(7) NFPA 801, *Standard for Fire Protection for Facilities Handling Radioactive Materials*, provides direction for controlling hazards associated with radioactive materials. NFPA 801 should be used only for issues related to radioactive materials in a laboratory. All other nonradioactive, laboratory issues are covered by NFPA 45.

A.1.3 See Figure A.1.3 for determining the applicability of NFPA 45 to a lab setting. Existing laboratories using chemicals that are not in compliance with this standard should be permitted to be continued being used if they provide protection to life and adjoining property that is equivalent to that in this standard.

A.3.2.1 Approved. The National Fire Protection Association does not approve, inspect, or certify any installations, procedures, equipment, or materials; nor does it approve or evaluate testing laboratories. In determining the acceptability of installations, procedures, equipment, or materials, the authority having jurisdiction may base acceptance on compliance with NFPA or other appropriate standards. In the absence of such standards, said authority may require evidence of proper installation, procedure, or use. The authority having jurisdiction may also refer to the listings or labeling practices of an organization that is concerned with product evaluations and is thus in a position to determine compliance with appropriate standards for the current production of listed items.

A.3.2.2 Authority Having Jurisdiction (AHJ). The phrase "authority having jurisdiction," or its acronym AHJ, is used in NFPA documents in a broad manner, since jurisdictions and approval agencies vary, as do their responsibilities. Where public safety is primary, the authority having jurisdiction may be a federal, state, local, or other regional department or individual such as a fire chief; fire marshal; chief of a fire prevention bureau, labor department, or health department; building official; electrical inspector; or others having statutory authority. For insurance purposes, an insurance inspection department, rating bureau, or other insurance company representative may be the authority having jurisdiction. In many circumstances, the property owner or his or her designated agent assumes the role of the authority having jurisdiction; at government installations, the commanding officer or departmental official may be the authority having jurisdiction.

A.3.2.4 Listed. The means for identifying listed equipment may vary for each organization concerned with product evaluation; some organizations do not recognize equipment as listed unless it is also labeled. The authority having jurisdic-

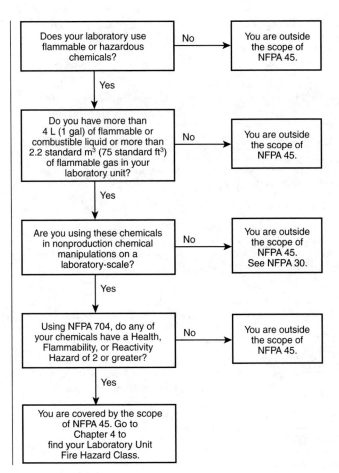

FIGURE A.1.3 Guide for Determining the Applicability of NFPA 45 to a Laboratory Setting.

tion should utilize the system employed by the listing organization to identify a listed product.

A.3.3.4 Biological Safety Cabinet. There are several types of biological safety cabinets.

Class II Type A1 cabinets (formerly designated Type A). Type A1 cabinets, which are not suitable for work with volatile toxic chemicals and volatile radionuclides, have the following characteristics:

(1) Maintain minimum average inflow velocity of 0.38 m/sec (75 ft/min) through the work access opening
(2) Have HEPA-filtered downflow air that is a portion of the mixed downflow and inflow air from a common plenum (i.e., a plenum from which a portion of the air is exhausted from the cabinet and the remainder supplied to the work area)
(3) Can exhaust HEPA-filtered air back into the laboratory or to the environment through an exhaust canopy
(4) Can have positive pressure contaminated ducts and plenums that are not surrounded by negative pressure plenums

Class II Type A2 cabinets (formerly designated Type B3). Type A2 cabinets used for work with minute quantities of volatile toxic chemicals and tracer amounts of radionuclides required as an adjunct to microbiological studies must be exhausted through

properly functioning exhaust canopies. Type A2 cabinets have the following characteristics:

(1) Maintain a minimum average inflow velocity of 0.5 m/sec (100 ft/min) through the work access opening
(2) Have HEPA-filtered downflow air that is a portion of the mixed downflow and inflow air from a common exhaust plenum
(3) Can exhaust HEPA-filtered air back into the laboratory or to the environment through an exhaust canopy
(4) Have all biologically contaminated ducts and plenums under negative pressure or surrounded by negative pressure ducts and plenums

Class II Type B1 cabinets. Type B1 cabinets can be used for work treated with minute quantities of volatile toxic chemicals and tracer amounts of radionuclides required as an adjunct to microbiological studies if work is done in the direct exhausted portion of the cabinet, or if the chemicals or radionuclides will not interfere with the work when recirculated in the downflow air. Type B1 cabinets have the following characteristics:

(1) Maintain a minimum average inflow velocity of 0.5 m/sec (100 ft/min) through the work access opening
(2) Have HEPA-filtered downflow air composed largely of uncontaminated recirculated inflow air
(3) Exhaust most of the contaminated downflow air through a dedicated duct exhausted to the atmosphere after passing through a HEPA filter
(4) Have all biologically contaminated ducts and plenums under negative pressure or surrounded by negative pressure ducts and plenums

Class II Type B2 cabinets (sometimes referred to as total exhaust). Type B2 cabinets can be used for work with volatile toxic chemicals and radionuclides required as an adjunct to microbiological studies. Type B2 cabinets have the following characteristics:

(1) Maintain a minimum average inflow velocity of 0.5 m/sec (100 ft/min) through the work access opening
(2) Have HEPA-filtered downflow air drawn from the laboratory or the outside air (i.e., downflow air is not recirculated from the cabinet exhaust air)
(3) Exhaust all inflow and downflow air to the atmosphere after filtration through a HEPA filter without recirculation in the cabinet or return to the laboratory
(4) Have all contaminated ducts and plenums under negative pressure, or surrounded by directly exhausted (nonrecirculated through the work area) negative pressure ducts and plenums

A.3.3.8 Chemical. For fire hazard ratings of many chemicals, see the NFPA's *Fire Protection Guide to Hazardous Materials*, which contains the following NFPA documents:

(1) NFPA 49, *Hazardous Chemicals Data*
(2) NFPA 325, *Guide to Fire Hazard Properties of Flammable Liquids, Gases, and Volatile Solids*

A.3.3.9 Chemical Fume Hood. For further information on descriptions of types of chemical fume hoods and exhaust ventilation devices, see ANSI/AIHA Z9.5, *Laboratory Ventilation*. The following are types of chemical fume hoods:

(1) *Conventional hood.* A square-post hood without an airfoil directional vane across the bottom of the hood face, and in most cases without provision for a bypass. As the sash is lowered in hoods without an air bypass, the face velocity increases rapidly. The square-post design and absence of a

deflector vane have been known to create turbulence at the hood face. The turbulence at the hood face can bring fumes from the hood interior out to the hood face, where they are easily drawn out into the room by the air turbulence caused by a person working at the hood, persons passing the hood, or minor room cross drafts. If hoods are not equipped with a bypass, face velocities could become objectionably high as the sash is closed, and with the sash completely closed, airflow can be insufficient to carry vapors away.

(2) *Bypass air hood.* A hood having a bypass protected by a grille that serves to maintain a relatively constant volume of airflow regardless of sash position. Current design recommends a streamlined entry profile with a deflector vane across the bottom of the hood to direct the airflow across the work surface.

(3) *Auxiliary air hood.* A bypass air hood with the addition of an auxiliary air bonnet to provide a direct source of makeup air in addition to the makeup air from the laboratory work area.

(4) Special purpose hoods are as follows:

   (a) *Radioisotope hoods.* Designed primarily for use with radiochemicals

   (b) *Perchloric acid hoods.* Designed primarily for use with perchloric acid

   (c) *Walk-in hoods.* Designed primarily for extra headroom to accommodate tall equipment

A.3.3.12 Cryogenic Fluid. See National Safety Council Data Sheet 1-688-86, *Cryogenic Fluids in the Laboratory.*

A.3.3.18 Face (of hood). This area is used to calculate the square footage of the hood opening, and face velocity is measured in this plane.

A.3.3.23 Flammable Solid. A chemical is considered to be a flammable solid if, when tested by the method described in 16 CFR 1500.44, it ignites and burns with a self-sustained flame at a rate greater than one-tenth of an inch per second along its major axis.

A.3.3.25 Health Care Facilities. Health care facilities include, but are not limited to, hospitals, nursing homes, limited care facilities, clinics, medical and dental offices, and ambulatory health care centers, whether permanent or movable. [**99,** 2005]

A.3.3.30 Inside Liquid Storage Area. Such areas include the following:

(1) *Inside a room.* A room totally enclosed within a building and having no exterior walls

(2) *Cut-off room.* A room within a building and having at least one exterior wall

(3) *Attached building.* A building having only one common wall with another building having other types of occupancies

(4) *Liquid warehouse.* A separate, detached building or attached building used for warehousing-type operations for liquids

A.3.3.38 Laboratory Work Area. This work area can be enclosed.

A.3.3.45.2 Educational Occupancy. Educational occupancies include academies, kindergartens, and schools. An educational occupancy is distinguished from an assembly occupancy in that the same occupants are regularly present.

A.3.3.45.4 Industrial Occupancy. See NFPA *101, Life Safety Code,* Chapter 40, for more information.

A.3.3.48 Oxidizer. Examples of other oxidizing gases include bromine, chlorine, or fluorine.

A.3.3.57 Storage Cabinet. Some local jurisdictions require bottom-venting of flammable liquids storage cabinets. Although this is not required by NFPA 30, *Flammable and Combustible Liquids Code,* some manufacturers provide plugged vent connections to accommodate these local jurisdictions.

A.3.3.59 Unattended Laboratory Operation. Absence for lunch, telephone calls, and so forth, without coverage by a knowledgeable person, constitutes an unattended laboratory operation.

A.4.2.1 The largest amounts of flammable and combustible liquids are permitted in Class A laboratory units, and the least amounts in Class D laboratory units.

A.4.3.1 For explosion hazard protection requirements, see Chapter 7.

A.4.3.1(3) For sources of data on chemical reactivity hazard and hazardous chemical reactions, see the NFPA's *Fire Protection Guide to Hazardous Materials,* which contains the following NFPA documents:

(1) NFPA 49, *Hazardous Chemicals Data*
(2) NFPA 325, *Guide to Fire Hazard Properties of Flammable Liquids, Gases, and Volatile Solids*
(3) NFPA 491, *Manual of Hazardous Chemical Reactions*

A.5.1.10 NFPA 90A, *Standard for the Installation of Air-Conditioning and Ventilating Systems,* requires that approved fire dampers be provided in all air-transfer openings in partitions required to have a fire resistance rating. The standard requires that approved fire dampers be provided where ducts or air grilles penetrate partitions required to have a fire resistance rating of 2 hours or more. Thus, although any air-transfer opening would have to be fire dampered in a required fire barrier of any rating, penetrations by ducts or air grilles would not have to be fire dampered if the required rating of the barrier is less than 2 hours.

A.5.4.1 A door to an adjoining laboratory work area or laboratory unit is considered to be a second means of access to an exit, provided that the laboratory unit is not of a higher fire hazard classification.

A.5.4.3 It should be noted that while doors swinging against egress and horizontally sliding doors are permitted in certain Class C and Class D laboratory work areas, NFPA *101, Life Safety Code,* and *NFPA 5000, Building Construction and Safety Code,* place limitations on their use based on number of occupants and area. Before doors swinging against egress and horizontally sliding doors are used, both NFPA *101* and *NFPA 5000* should be reviewed for requirements and limitations.

A.5.5 Modern laboratory design concepts provide a wide selection of laboratory furniture and equipment. Although such selections will be dictated by several factors, such as laboratory function, cost, serviceability, accessibility, repair, and so forth, any laboratory design should recognize and accommodate — to the extent practical — several needs directly related to improving the fire safety posture of the laboratory work area.

Casework design should be flexible to provide optimum use of storage capacity without interfering with the normal needs of the laboratory. This design can include desk areas that do not encourage underdesk storage, restraining techniques for items stored above eye level, ease of egress, provision for separation of incompatible chemicals or materials, provisions for ventilated or corrosion-resistant storage, or properly identified special facilities for unique waste storage needs, such as chemical, biological, or radioactive materials.

Easy access to laboratory utilities, such as piping, valves, and electrical switches and circuit-breaker panels, should be provided. All valves and switches should be properly identified in accordance with the governing codes and standards.

The use of slip-resistant floor surfaces should be considered.

A.6.2.3 It is suggested that automatic fire-extinguishing systems activate both a local audible alarm and an audible or visible alarm at a constantly attended location.

A.6.3.1 All laboratory buildings should be provided with standpipes and 3.8 cm (1½ in.) hose connections for use by trained occupants. Hose connections should be fitted with hose lines and combination straight stream–fog nozzles. Waterflow through the standpipe system should activate an audible fire alarm system on the premises.

A.6.6.2 Maintenance procedures should include inspection, testing, and maintenance of the following:

(1) Utilities (steam, gas, electrical)
(2) Air supply and exhaust systems
(3) Fire protection equipment
(4) Detectors and alarms
(5) Compressed gas regulators and pressure relief valves
(6) Waste disposal systems
(7) Fire doors
(8) Emergency lighting and exit signs
(9) Electrically operated equipment

A.6.6.3 An emergency response plan should be prepared and updated. The plan should be available for inspection by the AHJ, upon reasonable notice. The following information should be included in the emergency plan:

(1) The type of emergency equipment available and its location
(2) A brief description of any testing or maintenance programs for the available emergency equipment
(3) An indication that hazard identification marking is provided for each storage area
(4) Location of posted emergency response procedures
(5) Material safety data sheets (MSDSs) for all hazardous materials stored on site
(6) A list of responsible personnel who are designated and trained to be liaison personnel for the fire department; these individuals should be knowledgeable in the site emergency response procedures and should aid the emergency responders with the following functions:
    (a) Pre-emergency planning
    (b) Identifying where flammable, pyrophoric, oxidizing, and toxic gases are located
    (c) Accessing MSDSs
(7) A list of the types and quantities of compressed and liquefied gases normally at the facility

A.6.6.3.1(5) Unusual non-fire hazards that emergency response personnel might encounter in responding to a fire in a chemical laboratory might include the following:

(1) Poisons
(2) Corrosives
(3) Irritants
(4) Radioactivity
(5) Nonionizing radiation
(6) Biological hazards

Laboratory management should train emergency response personnel in detailed emergency response plans that address these special hazards.

Laboratory management should also encourage the public fire department to become familiar with these hazards through in-service inspections, joint emergency plan development, and coordinated emergency response drills.

Emergency telephones are of value when connected directly to an emergency office and when located within the laboratory building so that they can be readily used by laboratory personnel. They are also valuable when available at an exterior location for use by evacuees or passersby. An emergency telephone system should be interconnected with a mass notification system, such as a public address system.

The management of each laboratory work area covered by this standard should be responsible for developing and distributing an evacuation plan for the facility. The plan should be written with accompanying diagrams and distributed to each supervisor and posted in appropriate locations for all employees to read and study. In addition to fires and explosions, the evacuation plan should also consider hazardous incidents such as spills, leaks, or releases of flammable, toxic, or radioactive materials, and acts of nature such as tornadoes, hurricanes, and floods. The evacuation plan should include, but not be limited to, the following:

(1) Conditions under which evacuation will be necessary
(2) Method of alarm transmission
(3) Action to be taken by personnel upon receiving an alarm in addition to evacuation (e.g., turn off flames and other ignition sources)
(4) Primary and secondary routes to horizontal and vertical exits leading either to the exterior of the building or to safe refuge zones within the building, as might be permitted if total evacuation is not necessary and the alarm system is appropriately zoned
(5) Instructions necessary to prevent evacuees from hampering fire-fighting operations or essential duties of emergency personnel (i.e., move away from the building to a predesignated area)
(6) Accountability to determine if everyone has left the facility (Wardens or supervisors should be instructed to check all occupied spaces in their assigned area upon sounding of an alarm to ensure that everyone has heard the alarm and is evacuating. Personnel from particular groups, departments, floors, or areas should be instructed to gather in a predesignated area outside the building or in a safe refuge zone. Special procedures should be established for evacuation of handicapped persons. Wardens or supervisors should be responsible for accounting for all personnel in their areas, including guests and visitors.)
(7) Methods of notifying personnel as to when it is safe to re-enter the facility (Dependence on duly authorized persons, such as wardens, to pass this word will prevent someone from entering the facility prematurely.)

Laboratory management should conduct fire exit drills at least once a year to test the evacuation procedures by familiarizing personnel with exits, especially emergency exits not normally used, and the safe and efficient use of the exits. For required frequency of fire exit drills in educational occupancies and health care occupancies, see NFPA *101, Life Safety Code.* (Fire exit drills differ from fire drills in that the latter are held for purposes of fire-fighting practice by the fire brigade or other emergency organizations. Because a conflict exists between evacuation and fire fighting, management should appoint different persons to be responsible for each procedure, as one cannot effectively direct fire-fighting operations and evacuation simultaneously.)

Fire alarm systems, where available, should be used in the conduct of fire exit drills. No one should be excused from participating in a fire exit drill.

A.6.6.3.2 Laboratory personnel should be thoroughly indoctrinated in procedures to follow in cases of clothing fires. The most important instruction, one that should be stressed until it becomes second nature to all personnel, is to immediately drop to the floor and roll. All personnel should recognize that, in case of ignition of another person's clothing, they should immediately knock that person to the floor and roll that person around to smother the flames. Too often a person will panic and run if clothing ignites, resulting in more severe, often fatal, burn injuries.

Fire-retardant or flame-resistant clothing is one option available to help reduce the occurrence of clothing fires. Refer to NFPA 1975, *Standard on Station/Work Uniforms for Emergency Services*, for performance requirements and test methods for fire-resistant clothing.

It should be emphasized that use of safety showers, fire blankets, or fire extinguishers are of secondary importance. These items should be used only when immediately at hand. It should be recognized that rolling on the floor not only smothers the fire but also helps to keep flames out of the victim's face, reducing inhalation of smoke.

A.7.3(3) For further information on venting, see NFPA 68, *Standard on Explosion Protection by Deflagration Venting*.

A.7.5.3 A protective coating, such as mineral oil, can be applied to transparent sight panels exposed to corrosive vapors.

A.8.1 NFPA 90A, *Standard for the Installation of Air-Conditioning and Ventilating Systems*, and NFPA 91, *Standard for Exhaust Systems for Air Conveying of Vapors, Gases, Mists, and Noncombustible Particulate Solids*, contain additional requirements for general environmental ventilating systems.

A.8.2.1 For additional information on laboratory ventilation, see ANSI/AIHA Z9.5, *Laboratory Ventilation*. For information on preventing the spread of smoke by means of utilizing supply and exhaust systems to create airflows and pressure differences between rooms or building areas, see NFPA 92A, *Standard for Smoke-Control Systems Utilizing Barriers and Pressure Differences*.

A.8.2.2 It is not the intent of this standard to require emergency or standby power for laboratory ventilation systems.

A.8.2.3 Hoods having explosionproof electrical devices are sometimes referred to as *explosionproof hoods*. This term does not imply that they will contain an explosion, only that the electrical equipment will not provide a source of ignition.

A.8.3.2 Special studies such as air-dispersion modeling might be necessary to determine the location of air intakes for laboratories away from the influence of laboratory exhaust and other local point source emissions.

A.8.3.4 Room air current velocities in the vicinity of fume hoods should be as low as possible, ideally less than 30 percent of the face velocity of the fume hood. Air supply diffusion devices should be as far away from fume hoods as possible and have low exit velocities.

A.8.4.1 Ductless chemical fume hoods that pass air from the hood interior through an adsorption filter and then discharge the air into the laboratory are only applicable for use with nuisance vapors and dusts that do not present a fire or toxicity hazard.

A.8.4.2 Consideration should be made of the potential contamination of the fresh air supply by exhaust air containing vapors of flammable or toxic chemicals when using devices for energy conservation purposes.

A.8.4.4 Ducts should be sealed to prevent condensation, and so forth, from leaking into occupied areas.

A.8.4.7 Laboratory fume hood containment can be evaluated using the procedures contained in ASHRAE 110, *Method of Testing Performance of Laboratory Fume Hoods*. Face velocities of 0.4 m/sec to 0.6 m/sec (80 ft/min to 120 ft/min) generally provide containment if the hood location requirements and laboratory ventilation criteria of this standard are met.

In addition to maintaining proper fume hood face velocity, fume hoods that reduce the exhaust volume as the sash opening is reduced should maintain a minimum exhaust volume to ensure that contaminants are diluted and exhausted from a hood. The chemical fume hood exhaust airflow should not be reduced to less than the flow rate recommended in ANSI/AIHA Z9.5, *Laboratory Ventilation*.

A.8.4.9 Due to their low capture efficiency, canopy hoods should only be used for exhausting heat and nuisance odors and not for exhausting chemicals.

A.8.4.12 Exhaust stacks should extend at least 3 m (10 ft) above the highest point on the roof to protect personnel on the roof. Exhaust stacks might need to be much higher to dissipate effluent effectively, and studies might be necessary to determine adequate design. Related information on stack height can be found in Chapter 14, Airflow Around Buildings, of the ASHRAE *Handbook of Fundamentals*.

A.8.5.1 The designer of a laboratory exhaust system should consider the physical and chemical properties and hazard characteristics of the materials being conveyed. The exceptions cited recognize that some laboratory operations generate corrosive vapors that might attack available metallic duct materials. When it has been ascertained that metallic ducts will not withstand such an attack by the chemicals to be exhausted or where the unique nature of the work to be done mandates the use of nonmetallic ducts, nonmetallic ducts can be used. The designer should consider the use of chemical-resistant thermoplastic-lined metallic duct materials.

A.8.7.4 For informative material regarding spark-resistant fan construction, see Air Movement and Control Association (AMCA) Standards Handbook 99-0401-86, *Classifications for Spark Resistant Construction*.

A.8.7.6 Exhaust fans should be tested to ensure they do not rotate backward in new installations or after repair on motors.

A.8.8.1.1 Specifying the flame spread rating alone does not ensure that the liner will provide containment of a small fire.

A.8.8.1.2 Baffles normally should be adjusted for the best operating position for general use. Only where high heat loads or the routine use of large quantities of light or heavy gases occur should compensating adjustment be made. In most cases, however, the low concentrations of heavier-than-air and lighter-than-air vapors take on the characteristics of the large volumes of air going through the hood. It is recommended that the total adjustment not exceed 20 percent of the total airflow.

A.8.8.1.3 The means of containing minor spills might consist of a 6.4 mm (¼ in.) recess in the work surface, use of pans or trays, or creation of a recess by installing a curb across the front of the hood and sealing the joints between the work surface and the sides, back, and curb of the hood.

A.8.8.2 A hood sash greatly enhances the safety provided by a chemical fume hood, and it is recommended that the hood design incorporate this feature. For example, a hood sash can be adjusted to increase the face velocity when working on high hazard material. The sash can be used as a safety shield. It can be closed to contain a fire or runaway reaction, and it can be closed to contain experiments when the hood is left unattended.

Hoods without sashes or hoods with a side or rear sash in addition to a front sash do not offer the same degree of protection as do hoods with protected single face openings, and, thus, their use is not recommended. A small face opening can be desirable to save exhaust air and energy or to increase the maximum face velocity on existing hoods.

A.8.8.3 Users should be instructed and periodically reminded not to open sashes rapidly and to allow hood sashes to be open only when needed and only as much as necessary.

A.8.8.4 Locating services, controls, and electrical fixtures external to the hood minimizes the potential hazards of corrosion and arcing.

A.8.9.1 A person walking past the hood can create sufficient turbulence to disrupt a face velocity of 0.5 m/sec (100 ft/min). In addition, open windows or air impingement from an air diffuser can completely negate or dramatically reduce the face velocity and can also affect negative differential air pressure.

A.8.9.3 Place low hazard activities (such as desks and microscope benches) away from the chemical fume hood. The term *directly in front of* does not include those areas that are separated by a barrier such as a lab bench or other large structure that would serve as a shield.

A.8.10.1 A hazard and risk assessment should be conducted for fume hood operations. Circumstances exist where hood fire suppression systems might be appropriate as a stand-alone protection measure or as part of a more comprehensive strategy to reduce hazards and risks. This assessment should be reviewed when fume hood operations change. See the objectives of the standard stated in Section 1.2.

A.8.10.2(9) For further information, see the report entitled "An Investigation of Chemical Fume Hood Fire Protection Using Sprinkler and Water Mist Nozzles" prepared by Factory Mutual Research Corporation.

A.8.10.3.1 In 2001 at the University of California, a fire resulted in an injury and caused approximately $3.5 million in damage. Based on the investigation, it was concluded that the practice of not having fire dampers on the exhaust duct of the ventilation system at the shaft wall appears to have been beneficial in this fire scenario. The investigation observed that the exhaust system was effective at removing significant quantities of combustion products from the building during the fire, thereby reducing the amount of combustion products spreading to other areas of the building. The shutting down of the supply air by fire dampers did not significantly hinder the exhaust system because fresh air was provided though a broken window. However, if the window had not failed, the team concluded that the exhaust system probably would not have performed as well.

If protection of the openings is desired, one method is to use a subduct assembly. Where a branch duct connects to an enclosed exhaust riser located inside a shaft, which has a required fire resistance rating of 1 hour or more and in which the airflow moves upward, protection of the opening into the fire resistance–rated enclosure should be made with a steel subduct turned upward a minimum of 0.6 m (22 in.) in length and of a minimum thickness of 22 gauge [0.76 mm (0.030 in.)]. The steel subduct should be carried up inside the riser from each inlet duct penetration. This riser should be appropriately sized to accommodate the flow restriction created by the subduct.

A.8.10.7 Installation of sprinklers in the void area or in the chemical fume hood is an acceptable method to prevent flame spread.

A.8.11.1 If perchloric acid is heated above ambient temperature, it will give off vapors that can condense and form explosive perchlorates. Limited quantities of perchloric acid vapor can be kept from condensing in laboratory exhaust systems by trapping or scrubbing the vapors at the point of origin. Scrubbing systems have been described in published articles.

A.8.11.8 Perchloric acid hoods should be washed down after each use.

A.8.11.10 A simple and sensitive test for perchlorates is available that uses a 0.3 percent solution of methylene blue in water. A few drops of the test solution in a small quantity [about 25 mL (0.84 oz)] of water washed from the duct to be tested will produce a violet precipitate if perchlorates are present. Approximately 12 mg (0.00042 oz) of perchlorate in this volume [500 mg/L (0.067 oz/gal)] can be recognized easily as a positive test. Because the methylene blue test can produce false negatives and false positives, as shown in "Returning Perchlorate-Contaminated Fume Hood Systems to Service, Part II" (Bader et al.), a more specific and quantifiable method for perchlorates is available that uses a perchlorate ion selective electrode. Several methods were compared in "Returning Perchlorate-Contaminated Fume Hood Systems to Service, Part I" (Phillips et al.) and in *Perchloric Acid and Perchlorates* (Schilt).

An effective method for washing down ductwork suspected of perchlorate contamination has been recommended in the CRC *Handbook of Laboratory Safety*. The method uses steaming of the ducts for 24 hours to condense water on all surfaces and dissolve and wash away perchlorate deposits. If tests after 24 hours show perchlorates in the final wash water, the steaming should be continued for another 24 hours until the test is negative. Where radiation contamination is present, in other than airtight ductwork, a continuous washdown or use of steam methods should not be done unless all the exhaust system is made airtight.

A.8.12.1 Laboratory hoods in which radioactive materials are handled should be identified with the radiation hazard symbol. For information, see NFPA 801, *Standard for Fire Protection for Facilities Handling Radioactive Materials.*

A.8.13.1 The operating characteristics of some chemical fume hood designs, particularly auxiliary air chemical fume hoods, change at intermediate positions of sash height. It is, therefore, important to verify inward airflow over the face of the hood according to 8.13.1(5) at several sash heights from full open to closed.

A number of test procedures for verifying performance of chemical fume hoods that have been installed in the field have been published.

A test procedure is given in *Standard on Laboratory Fume Hoods*, by The Scientific Equipment and Furniture Association (SEFA), that uses a velometer and visible fume for checking hood performance.

A standard has been issued by the American Society of Heating, Refrigerating, and Air Conditioning Engineers entitled ASHRAE 110, *Method of Testing Performance of Laboratory Fume Hoods.*

The Environmental Protection Agency's *Procedure for Certifying Laboratory Fume Hoods to Meet EPA Standards* contains a test procedure utilizing sulfur hexafluoride as a test gas.

A.8.13.5.1 The annual inspection of air supply and exhaust fans, motors, and components should ensure that equipment is clean, dry, tight, and friction-free. Bearings should be properly lubricated on a regular basis, according to manufacturers' recommendations. Protective devices should be checked to ensure that settings are correct and that ratings have been tested under simulated overload conditions. Inspections should be made by personnel familiar with the manufacturers' instructions and equipped with proper instruments, gauges, and tools.

A.9.1 Before a hazardous chemical is ordered, controls should be established to ensure that adequate facilities and procedures are available for receiving, storing, using, and disposing of the material. Information sources include the following NFPA documents, which are contained in NFPA's *Fire Protection Guide to Hazardous Materials*:

(1) NFPA 49, *Hazardous Chemicals Data*
(2) NFPA 325, *Guide to Fire Hazard Properties of Flammable Liquids, Gases, and Volatile Solids*
(3) NFPA 491, *Manual of Hazardous Chemical Reactions*

A.9.2.2.1 The route used to transport hazardous materials between receiving rooms, storage rooms, dispensing rooms, and laboratory units of a facility should be appropriate to both the quantity and characteristics of the material being transported. Where possible, heavy or bulky quantities of hazardous materials should be transported by elevator, preferably one reserved exclusively for freight. In any event, the transport of hazardous materials in any quantity on an elevator should be accomplished by the minimum number of persons necessary to accomplish the task safely. All other persons should be excluded from an elevator while hazardous materials are present. Use of stairways for transport of small quantities of hazardous materials should be minimized.

A.9.2.2.2 Some common construction materials are subject to serious corrosion or formation of explosive compounds if used for or contacted by certain chemicals and gases commonly used in the laboratory. For example, copper tubing forms explosive compounds if it is used to pipe acetylene; azide salts are not compatible with copper or lead piping; mercury amalgamates in lead pipes.

Thermoplastic pipe used in chemical service, such as in laboratory waste drains, will frequently soften even when not directly attacked by chemical solvents. When this happens, much of the original strength and rigidity of the pipe is lost. If installed above ground or floor level, such piping should be provided with adequate rack support to prevent sagging. Burying plastic pipe used for chemical waste is not recommended

because normal expansion might cause the pipe to collapse if the pipe has been softened by solvent attack.

A.9.2.3.1 This section establishes maximum allowable quantities of hazardous materials for individual laboratory units based upon reference to the locally adopted building and/or fire code. It is the intent of the Committee to draw a correlation between the term *laboratory unit* used in NFPA 45 and other terms such as *control area* or *laboratory suite*, which are typically used in locally adopted building and fire codes. For example, if the locally adopted building code utilizes a control area methodology, the maximum allowable quantities of hazardous materials for an individual laboratory unit would be equal to the baseline maximum quantities established for a control area. The maximum quantities of flammable and combustible liquids in a laboratory unit might then need to be modified based upon the application of Table 10.1.1(a) and Table 10.1.1(b).

A.9.2.3.2 For guidance, see NFPA's *Fire Protection Guide to Hazardous Materials*, which contains NFPA 49, *Hazardous Chemicals Data*, and NFPA 491, *Manual of Hazardous Chemical Reactions.*

A.9.2.3.4 There are several chemicals that can increase in hazard potential if subjected to long-term storage. Time alone can be only partially responsible, depending on the specific chemical. For example, exposure to air or light can cause the formation of highly shock-sensitive or friction-sensitive peroxides. Some hygroscopic or water-reactive compounds, such as metallic sodium, can autoignite on exposure to air or moisture. Another example is picric acid, which becomes highly shock-sensitive when its normal water content is allowed to evaporate. Reactive monomers that have been inhibited to reduce the chance of unintentional polymerization can become unstable when the inhibitor is consumed.

Such chemicals as described in 9.2.3.4 and A.9.2.3.4, which can increase in hazard potential over time, are common to chemical laboratories and are routinely handled without incident. Still, the user should use appropriate reference material to adequately assess the often multiple hazards associated with the use of chemicals.

A.9.2.3.4.1 Managing time-sensitive chemicals might be perceived as being complex. For help in determining what chemicals are time-sensitive, their inspection periods, inspection methodologies, and pass/fail criteria for these inspections, see one of the two sources by Bailey et al. or the source by Quigley et al.

A.9.2.3.5 See NFPA 30, *Flammable and Combustible Liquids Code*, for performance-based requirements if storage cabinets are vented for any reason.

A.10.1.2 Transferring flammable liquids from 1 gal– or 4 L–sized glass shipping containers to metal containers is a relatively expensive and hazardous operation. Such practices are not considered prudent, and are not recommended or required by NFPA for fire protection in laboratories using chemicals.

NFPA 45 allows glass containers in accordance with 10.1.2(1).

Class IA and IB flammable liquids in glass containers larger than the 500 mL (1 pt) and 1 L (1 qt) sizes permitted by Table 10.1.2 should be kept in containers of sufficient size to hold the contents of the glass containers.

The presence of flammable liquids in glass containers presents substantial hazards from accidental breakage. Many suppliers furnish glass containers with shatter-resistant coatings. These shatter-resistant glass containers offer significant protection from accidental breakage and are recommended for use when hazardous chemicals need to be kept in glass rather than plastic or metal containers.

A.10.3.1 Ventilation for dispensing operations should be provided to prevent overexposure of personnel dispensing flammable liquids. Control of solvent vapors is most effective if local exhaust ventilation is provided at or close to the point of transfer. Explosion venting is not required for separate inside liquid storage areas if containers are no greater than 227 L (60 gal) and if dispensing from containers larger than 4 L (1 gal) is by means of approved pumps or other devices drawing through a top opening. Movement of liquid to or from equipment in a closed system is not subject to this requirement.

A.10.3.2 Where practicable, dispensing operations should be separated from the storage of flammable and combustible liquids because of the exposure of greater quantities to the hazards of dispensing operations. Movement of liquid to or from equipment in a closed system is not subject to this requirement.

A.10.3.3 The requirement permits the use of squeeze bottles in laboratories. Their use greatly reduces spills, while aiding in accurately dispensing liquids onto small components or surfaces. The small rate of intermittent discharge through a squeeze bottle's discharge tube has not proven to be a hazard over many years of use.

In laboratory occupancies where pouring from and filling of laboratory-size containers is performed within a laboratory fume hood or other similarly ventilated enclosure or space, ignition due to static discharge is not likely to occur. This might be attributed to a combination of factors such as the following:

(1) Smaller size containers than those used in industrial or commercial occupancies
(2) Low flow rates during manual pouring/ filling
(3) Ventilation to below the lower flammable limits
(4) Contact made between containers (Good laboratory technique dictates that liquids be poured down the side of the container or by use of a stirring rod, thus avoiding splashing or turbulence.)

Perhaps of some yet-to-be-determined significance is the undefined charge transfer mechanism that can take place between nonconductive containers or between containers and the person performing the transfer. (For information on methods to reduce static electricity, see NFPA 77, *Recommended Practice on Static Electricity*.)

A.10.4.3 Relief discharge to a laboratory exhaust might not be appropriate for all sizes of containers for all solvents. Not all lab hoods and exhaust systems are constructed the same and might not be capable of containing or withstanding the vented vapors. Many fume hoods contain ignition sources. The user should evaluate each system based on the use.

A.10.4.6 Examples of these methods include, but are not limited to, a dead man valve or a remotely actuated valve on the liquid line or removal of the pressure being applied.

A.10.5.3 The requirements of 10.5.3 can be accomplished by either of the following:

(1) Limiting the temperatures of internal heated surfaces that can be exposed to the vapors to no more than 80 percent of the autoignition temperature of the material being heated

(2) Providing mechanical exhaust ventilation that discharges to a safe location to keep the concentration of flammable gas or vapor below 25 percent of the lower flammable limit (The ventilation equipment should be interlocked with the heating system so that heating cannot take place unless the ventilation system is operating.)

Also, any electrical equipment located within the outer shell, within the compartment, on the door, or on the door frame should be suitable for Class I, Division 1 hazardous (classified) locations and any electrical equipment mounted on the outside of the equipment should be as follows:

(1) Suitable for Class I, Division 2 hazardous (classified) locations
(2) Installed on the outside surface of the equipment where exposure to vapors will be minimal

Consideration should also be given to providing deflagration venting, as described in NFPA 86, *Standard for Ovens and Furnaces*.

A.11.1.2 Cylinders of hydrogen fluoride and hydrogen bromide should be returned to the supplier within 2 years of the shipping date.

Cylinders of corrosive or unstable gases should be returned to the supplier when the expiration date of the maximum recommended retention period has been reached. Examples of such corrosive or unstable gases include the following:

(1) Acid and alkaline gases
(2) Gases subject to autopolymerization
(3) Gases subject to explosive decomposition

Cylinders not in active use should be removed from laboratory work areas to a storage facility, as described in CGA Pamphlet P-1, *Safe Handling of Compressed Gases in Containers*. In the absence of a maximum recommended retention time, a 36-month interval should be used.

A.11.1.3 Such vessels cannot be used in commerce unless DOT approved.

A.11.2.1 For additional information, see the following:

(1) CGA Pamphlet P-1, *Safe Handling of Compressed Gases in Containers*
(2) ASME B31.1, *Power Piping* (including addendum)
(3) ASME B31.3, *Process Piping*
(4) National Safety Council Data Sheet 1-688-86, *Cryogenic Fluids in the Laboratory*

A.11.2.3 Additional shutoff valves, located in accessible locations outside of the areas in which the gases are used, are acceptable.

A.11.2.5 It is recommended that each intermediate regulator and valve also be identified. The identification should conform to ANSI A13.1, *Scheme for the Identification of Piping Systems*.

A.11.2.6 Great care should be taken when converting a piping system from one gas to another. In addition to the requirements of 11.2.6, thorough cleaning to remove residues might be essential. For example, inert oil-pumped nitrogen will leave a combustible organic residue that is incompatible with oxygen and other oxidizing agents. Similar incompatibilities can occur with other materials.

A.11.4.1.2 Air can be condensed when it contacts containers or piping containing cryogenic fluids. When this occurs, the concentration of oxygen in the condensed air increases, thereby increasing the likelihood of ignition of organic material.

A.12.1.1 Reference sources include the following, contained in NFPA's *Fire Protection Guide to Hazardous Materials*:

(1) NFPA 49, *Hazardous Chemicals Data*
(2) NFPA 325, *Guide to Fire Hazard Properties of Flammable Liquids, Gases, and Volatile Solids*
(3) NFPA 491, *Manual of Hazardous Chemical Reactions*

A.12.1.1.4 When a new chemical is produced, it should be subjected to a hazard analysis as appropriate to the reasonably anticipated hazard characteristics of the material. Such tests might include, but are not limited to, differential thermal analysis, accelerating rate calorimetry, drop weight shock sensitivity, autoignition temperature, flash point, thermal stability under containment, heat of combustion, and other appropriate tests.

A.12.1.4 Protection against ignition sources associated with typical laboratory apparatus can be achieved by distance, pressurization of motor or switch housings, or inerting techniques that can effectively prevent flammable vapor concentrations from contacting ignition sources. (See NFPA 496, *Standard for Purged and Pressurized Enclosures for Electrical Equipment*, for requirements for purge systems for electrical enclosures, and NFPA 69, *Standard on Explosion Prevention Systems*, for requirements for inerting systems.)

A.12.1.6.4 Procedures might include chilling, quenching, cutoff of reactant supply, venting, dumping, and "short-stopping" or inhibiting.

A.12.2.2.1 Figure A.12.2.2.1 gives examples of labels that can be used on laboratory refrigerators.

> Do not store flammable solvents in this refrigerator.

Label used for unmodified domestic models

> Notice: This is not an explosionproof refrigerator, but it has been designed to permit safe storage of materials producing flammable vapors. Containers should be well-stoppered or tightly closed.

Label for laboratory-safe or modified domestic models

FIGURE A.12.2.2.1 Labels to Be Used in Laboratory Refrigerators.

A.12.2.2.2 Protection against the ignition of flammable vapors in refrigerated equipment is available through three types of laboratory refrigerators: explosionproof, "laboratory-safe" (or "explosion-safe"), and modified domestic models.

Explosionproof refrigeration equipment is designed to protect against ignition of flammable vapors both inside and outside the refrigerated storage compartment. This type is intended and recommended for environments such as pilot plants or laboratory work areas where all electrical equipment is required to meet the requirements of Article 501 of *NFPA 70, National Electrical Code*.

The design concepts of the "explosion-safe" or "laboratory-safe" type of refrigerator are based on the typical laboratory environment. The primary intent is to eliminate ignition of vapors inside the storage compartment by sources also within the com-

partment. In addition, commercially available "laboratory-safe" refrigerators incorporate such design features as thresholds, self-closing doors, friction latches or magnetic door gaskets, and special materials for the inner shell. All of these features are intended to control or limit the damage should an exothermic reaction occur within the storage compartment. Finally, the compressor and its circuits and controls are located at the top of the unit to further reduce the potential for ignition of floor-level vapors. In general, the design features of a commercially available "laboratory-safe" refrigerator are such that they provide important safeguards not easily available through modification of domestic models.

A.12.2.2.2.1 The use of domestic refrigerators for the storage of typical laboratory solvents presents a significant hazard to the laboratory work area. Refrigerator temperatures are almost universally higher than the flash points of the flammable liquids most often stored in them. In addition to vapor accumulation, a domestic refrigerator contains readily available ignition sources, such as thermostats, light switches, and heater strips, all within or exposed to the refrigerated storage compartment. Furthermore, the compressor and its circuits are typically located at the bottom of the unit, where vapors from flammable liquid spills or leaks could easily accumulate.

Although not considered optimum protection, it is possible to modify domestic refrigerators to achieve some degree of protection. However, the modification process can be applied only to manual defrost refrigerators; the self-defrosting models cannot be successfully modified to provide even minimum safeguards against vapor ignition. The minimum procedures for modification include the following:

(1) Relocation of manual temperature controls to the exterior of the storage compartment, sealing all points where capillary tubing or wiring formerly entered the storage compartment
(2) Removal of light switches and light assemblies and sealing of all resulting openings
(3) Replacement of positive mechanical door latches with magnetic door gaskets

Regardless of the approach used (explosionproof, "laboratory-safe," modified domestic, or unmodified domestic), every laboratory refrigerator should be clearly marked to indicate whether it is safe for storage of flammable materials. Internal laboratory procedures should ensure that laboratory refrigerators are being properly used.

A.12.2.5.1 Pressure vessels require specialized design beyond the scope of normal workshop practice. For design of pressure vessels, see Section VIII, "Rules for Construction of Pressure Vessels," Division 1, ASME *Boiler and Pressure Vessel Code*.

A.13.1.1 Examples of severe or unusual hazards that might require posting of signs include the following:

(1) Unstable chemicals
(2) Radioactive chemicals
(3) Carcinogens, mutagens, and teratogens
(4) Pathogens
(5) High-pressure reactions
(6) High-powered lasers
(7) Water-reactive materials
(8) Cryogens

Also, the names and home telephone numbers of one or more persons working in each laboratory work area should be posted at the entrance to that work area. Such information should be kept current.

It is important to recognize that an extremely toxic substance need not be identified as a proportionately hazardous substance. The quantity of the substance, the ease of penetration of its container or risk of its release by fire, and the probability of harming emergency response personnel are the true measures of the hazard level. This standard does not exclusively endorse any particular convention for communicating unusual hazards to emergency response personnel, recognizing that professional judgments need to be made on a facility-by-facility basis. These judgments should recognize several existing conventions.

Use of the system presented in NFPA 704, *Standard System for the Identification of the Hazards of Materials for Emergency Response*, which might be suitable for flammable liquid storage cabinets or those laboratories containing a nearly constant chemical inventory, is not recommended for multichemical laboratories where the chemicals can change frequently. Such laboratories can include any of the following:

(1) Analytical, biological (public health, genetic engineering, bacteriological)
(2) Physical and chemical (organic, inorganic, physical, research, crystallographic, forensic)
(3) Instructional (college and high school chemistry and physics laboratories)
(4) Metallurgical
(5) Mineralogical
(6) Fine art restoration and identification
(7) Dental

Even where storage within a laboratory involves unusually high amounts of flammable or toxic or reactive materials (and hence calls for hazard identification), a lettered sign is generally more easily understood than a numerical designation. Hence, the NFPA 704 system is not recommended for laboratories in general.

A.13.2 The exhaust system should be identified "WARNING — Chemical Laboratory Exhaust" (or "Chemical Fume Hood Exhaust" or other appropriate wording). Exhaust system discharge stacks and discharge vents and exhaust system fans should be marked to identify the laboratories or work areas being served.

Annex B Supplementary Definitions

This annex is not a part of the requirements of this NFPA document but is included for informational purposes only.

B.1 NFPA 30 Definitions. The following definitions are extracted from NFPA 30, *Flammable and Combustible Liquids Code*.

B.1.1 Flammable Liquid. Any liquid that has a closed-cup flash point below 100°F (37.8°C), as determined by the test procedures and apparatus set forth in NFPA 30, Section 4.4, and a Reid vapor pressure that does not exceed an absolute pressure of 40 psi (276 kPa) at 100°F (37.8°C), as determined by ASTM D 323, *Standard Test Method for Vapor Pressure of Petroleum Products (Reid Method)*. [**30**, 2008]

B.1.2 Classification of Flammable Liquids. Class I liquids shall be further subclassified in accordance with the following:

(1) Class IA Liquid — Any liquid that has a flash point below 73°F (22.8°C) and a boiling point below 100°F (37.8°C)

(2) Class IB Liquid — Any liquid that has a flash point below 73°F (22.8°C) and a boiling point at or above 100°F (37.8°C)
(3) Class IC Liquid — Any liquid that has a flash point at or above 73°F (22.8°C), but below 100°F (37.8°C)

[**30**:4.3.1]

B.1.3 Combustible Liquid. Any liquid that has a closed-cup flash point at or above 100°F (37.8°C), as determined by the test procedures and apparatus set forth in NFPA 30, Section 4.4. [**30**, 2008]

B.1.4 Classification of Combustible Liquids. Combustible liquids shall be classified in accordance with the following:

(1) Class II Liquid — Any liquid that has a flash point at or above 100°F (37.8°C) and below 140°F (60°C)
(2) Class III Liquid — Any liquid that has a flash point at or above 140°F (60°C)

    (a) Class IIIA Liquid — Any liquid that has a flash point at or above 140°F (60°C), but below 200°F (93°C)
    (b) Class IIIB — Any liquid that has a flash point at or above 200°F (93°C)

[**30**,4.3.2]

B.2 NFPA 704 Definitions. The following definitions are extracted from NFPA 704, *Standard System for the Identification of the Hazards of Materials for Emergency Response*.

B.2.1 Health Hazard. Health hazard ratings shall address the capability of a material to cause personal injury due to contact with or entry into the body via inhalation, ingestion, skin contact, or eye contact. [**704**:5.1.1]

The degrees of health hazard shall be ranked according to the probable severity of the effects of exposure to emergency response personnel detailed in Table B.2.1. [**704**:5.2]

B.2.2 Flammability Hazards. Flammability hazards ratings shall address the degree of susceptibility of materials to burning [**704**:6.1.1]. Because many materials will burn under one set of conditions but will not burn under others, the form or condition of the material shall be considered, along with its inherent properties. [**704**:6.1.2]

B.2.3 Degrees of Hazard. The degrees of flammability hazard shall be ranked according to the susceptibility of materials to burning as detailed in Table B.2.3. [**704**:6.2]

B.2.4 Instability Hazards.

B.2.4.1 This [section] shall address the degree of instrinsic susceptibility of materials to release energy [**704**:7.1.1], [and] those materials capable of rapidly releasing energy by themselves, through self-reaction or polymerization. [**704**:7.1.1.1]

B.2.4.2 The violence of a reaction or decomposition can be increased by heat or pressure…[or] by mixing with other materials to form fuel–oxidizer combinations, or by contact with incompatible substances, sensitizing contaminants, or catalysts. [**704**: A.7.1.1]

B.2.4.3 Because of the wide variations of unintentional combinations possible in fire or other emergencies, these extraneous hazard factors (except for the effect of water) shall not be applied to a general numerical rating of hazards. Where large quantities of materials are stored together, inadvertent mixing shall be considered in order to establish appropriate separation or isolation. [**704**:7.1.2]

The NFPA 704 ratings are applied to numerous chemicals in the NFPA *Fire Protection Guide to Hazardous Materials*, which contains withdrawn standards NFPA 49, *Hazardous Chemicals Data*, and NFPA 325, *Guide to Fire Hazard Properties of Flammable*

Table B.2.1 Degrees of Health Hazards

Degree of Hazard*	Criteria
4 — Materials that, under emergency conditions, can be lethal	Gases whose LC_{50} for acute inhalation toxicity is less than or equal to 1000 parts per million (ppm) Any liquid whose saturated vapor concentration at 20°C (68°F) is equal to or greater than ten times its LC_{50} for acute inhalation toxicity, if its LC_{50} is less than or equal to 1000 ppm Dusts and mists whose LC_{50} for acute inhalation toxicity is less than or equal to 0.5 milligrams per liter (mg/L) Materials whose LD_{50} for acute dermal toxicity is less than or equal to 40 milligrams per kilogram (mg/kg) Materials whose LD_{50} for acute oral toxicity is less than or equal to 5 mg/kg
3 — Materials that, under emergency conditions, can cause serious or permanent injury	Gases whose LC_{50} for acute inhalation toxicity is greater than 1000 ppm but less than or equal to 3000 ppm Any liquid whose saturated vapor concentration at 20°C (68°F) is equal to or greater than its LC_{50} for acute inhalation toxicity, if its LC_{50} is less than or equal to 3000 ppm and that does not meet the criteria for degree of hazard 4 Dusts and mists whose LC_{50} for acute inhalation toxicity is greater than 0.5 mg/L but less than or equal to 2 mg/L Materials whose LD_{50} for acute dermal toxicity is greater than 40 mg/kg but less than or equal to 200 mg/kg Materials that are corrosive to the respiratory tract Materials that are corrosive to the eye or cause irreversible corneal opacity Materials that are corrosive to skin Cryogenic gases that cause frostbite and irreversible tissue damage Compressed liquefied gases with boiling points at or below −55°C (−66.5°F) that cause frostbite and irreversible tissue damage Materials whose LD_{50} for acute oral toxicity is greater than 5 mg/kg but less than or equal to 50 mg/kg
2 — Materials that, under emergency conditions, can cause temporary incapacitation or residual injury	Gases whose LC_{50} for acute inhalation toxicity is greater than 3000 ppm but less than or equal to 5000 ppm Any liquid whose saturated vapor concentration at 20°C (68°F) is equal to or greater than one-fifth its LC_{50} for acute inhalation toxicity, if its LC_{50} is less than or equal to 5000 ppm and that does not meet the criteria for either degree of hazard 3 or degree of hazard 4 Dusts and mists whose LC_{50} for acute inhalation toxicity is greater than 2 mg/L but less than or equal to 10 mg/L Materials whose LD_{50} for acute dermal toxicity is greater than 200 mg/kg but less than or equal to 1000 mg/kg Compressed liquefied gases with boiling points between −30°C (−22°F) and −55°C (−66.5°F) that can cause severe tissue damage, depending on duration of exposure Materials that are respiratory irritants Materials that cause severe but reversible irritation to the eyes or lacrimators Materials that are primary skin irritants or sensitizers Materials whose LD_{50} for acute oral toxicity is greater than 50 mg/kg but less than or equal to 500 mg/kg
1 — Materials that, under emergency conditions, can cause significant irritation	Gases and vapors whose LC_{50} for acute inhalation toxicity is greater than 5000 ppm but less than or equal to 10,000 ppm Dusts and mists whose LC_{50} for acute inhalation toxicity is greater than 10 mg/L but less than or equal to 200 mg/L Materials whose LD_{50} for acute dermal toxicity is greater than 1000 mg/kg but less than or equal to 2000 mg/kg Materials that cause slight to moderate irritation to the respiratory tract, eyes, and skin Materials whose LD_{50} for acute oral toxicity is greater than 500 mg/kg but less than or equal to 2000 mg/kg
0 — Materials that, under emergency conditions, would offer no hazard beyond that of ordinary combustible materials	Gases and vapors whose LC_{50} for acute inhalation toxicity is greater than 10,000 ppm Dusts and mists whose LC_{50} for acute inhalation toxicity is greater than 200 mg/L Materials whose LD_{50} for acute dermal toxicity is greater than 2000 mg/kg Materials whose LD_{50} for acute oral toxicity is greater than 2000 mg/kg Materials that are essentially nonirritating to the respiratory tract, eyes, and skin

*For each degree of hazard, the criteria are listed in a priority order based upon the likelihood of exposure.
[**704:** Table 5.2]

| Table B.2.3 Degrees of Flammability Hazards |

Degree of Hazard	Criteria
4 — Materials that will rapidly or completely vaporize at atmospheric pressure and normal ambient temperature or that are readily dispersed in air and will burn readily.	Flammable gases. Flammable cryogenic materials. Any liquid or gaseous material that is liquid while under pressure and has a flash point below 22.8°C (73°F) and a boiling point below 37.8°C (100°F) (i.e., Class IA liquids). Materials that ignite spontaneously when exposed to air. Solids containing greater than 0.5 percent by weight of a flammable or combustible solvent are rated by the closed cup flash point of the solvent.
3 — Liquids and solids that can be ignited under almost all ambient temperature conditions. Materials in this degree produce hazardous atmospheres with air under almost all ambient temperatures or, though unaffected by ambient temperatures, are readily ignited under almost all conditions.	Liquids having a flash point below 22.8°C (73°F) and a boiling point at or above 37.8°C (100°F) and those liquids having a flash point at or above 22.8°C (73°F) and below 37.8°C (100°F) (i.e., Class IB and Class IC liquids). Finely divided solids, typically less than 75 micrometers (µm) (200 mesh), that present an elevated risk of forming an ignitible dust cloud, such as finely divided sulfur, *National Electrical Code* Group E dusts (e.g., aluminum, zirconium, and titanium), and bis-phenol A. Materials that burn with extreme rapidity, usually by reason of self-contained oxygen (e.g., dry nitrocellulose and many organic peroxides). Solids containing greater than 0.5 percent by weight of a flammable or combustible solvent are rated by the closed cup flash point of the solvent.
2 — Materials that must be moderately heated or exposed to relatively high ambient temperatures before ignition can occur. Materials in this degree would not under normal conditions form hazardous atmospheres with air, but under high ambient temperatures or under moderate heating could release vapor in sufficient quantities to produce hazardous atmospheres with air.	Liquids having a flash point at or above 37.8°C (100°F) and below 93.4°C (200°F) (i.e., Class II and Class IIIA liquids). Finely divided solids less than 420 µm (40 mesh) that present an ordinary risk of forming an ignitible dust cloud. Solid materials in a flake, fibrous, or shredded form that burn rapidly and create flash fire hazards, such as cotton, sisal, and hemp. Solids and semisolids that readily give off flammable vapors. Solids containing greater than 0.5 percent by weight of a flammable or combustible solvent are rated by the closed cup flash point of the solvent.
1 — Materials that must be preheated before ignition can occur. Materials in this degree require considerable preheating, under all ambient temperature conditions, before ignition and combustion can occur.	Materials that will burn in air when exposed to a temperature of 815.5°C (1500°F) for a period of 5 minutes in accordance with ASTM D 6668, *Standard Test Method for the Discrimination Between Flammability Ratings of F = 0 and F = 1.* Liquids, solids, and semisolids having a flash point at or above 93.4°C (200°F) (i.e., Class IIIB liquids). Liquids with a flash point greater than 35°C (95°F) that do not sustain combustion when tested using the *Method of Testing for Sustained Combustibility*, per 49 CFR 173, Appendix H, or the UN publications *Recommendations on the Transport of Dangerous Goods* and *Manual of Tests and Criteria.* Liquids with a flash point greater than 35°C (95°F) in a water-miscible solution or dispersion with a water noncombustible liquid/solid content of more than 85 percent by weight. Liquids that have no fire point when tested by ASTM D 92, *Standard Test Method for Flash and Fire Points by Cleveland Open Cup*, up to the boiling point of the liquid or up to a temperature at which the sample being tested shows an obvious physical change. Combustible pellets, powders, and granules greater than 420 µm (40 mesh). Finely divided solids less than 420 µm that are nonexplosible in air at ambient conditions, such as low volatile carbon black and polyvinylchloride (PVC). Most ordinary combustible materials. Solids containing greater than 0.5 percent by weight of a flammable or combustible solvent are rated by the closed cup flash point of the solvent.
0 — Materials that will not burn under typical fire conditions, including intrinsically noncombustible materials such as concrete, stone, and sand	Materials that will not burn in air when exposed to a temperature of 816°C (1500°F) for a period of 5 minutes in accordance with Annex D [of NFPA 704]

[**704**:Table 6.2]

Liquids, Gases, and Volatile Solids. These were withdrawn as NFPA standards (and are therefore no longer published in the *National Fire Codes®*). However, they are maintained by NFPA staff in a database that will be available to the public electronically in the future and in updates of the NFPA *Fire Protection Guide to Hazardous Materials.* The Committee wished to note that the documents were withdrawn solely for expediency in updating the data, which was not possible in a 3- to 5-year revision cycle. [**704:** A.4.2.2]

B.2.4.4 The degree of instability hazard shall indicate to firefighting and emergency personnel whether the area shall be evacuated, whether a fire shall be fought from a protected location, whether caution shall be used in approaching a spill or fire to apply extinguishing agents, or whether a fire can be fought using normal procedures. [**704:**7.1.3]

B.2.4.5 Definitions.

B.2.4.5.1 Stable Materials. Those materials that normally have the capacity to resist changes in their chemical composition, despite exposure to air, water, and heat as encountered in fire emergencies. [**704,** 2007]

B.2.4.5.2 Unstable Materials. A material that, in the pure state or as commercially produced, will vigorously polymerize, decompose or condense, become self-reactive, or otherwise undergo a violent chemical change under conditions of shock, pressure, or temperature. [**704,** 2007]

B.2.5 Degrees of Hazard. The degrees of hazard shall be ranked according to ease, rate, and quantity of energy release of the material in pure or commercial form detailed in Table B.2.5. [**704,** 7.2]

Annex C Supplementary Information on Explosion Hazards and Protection

This annex is not a part of the requirements of this NFPA document but is included for informational purposes only.

C.1 Scope. This annex is intended to provide laboratory management with information to assist in understanding the potential consequences of an explosion and the need for adequately designed protection. It is not intended to be a design manual.

C.2 Explosion. An explosion is the bursting or rupture of an enclosure or a container due to the development of internal pressure from a deflagration. [69, 2008] Reactive explosions are further categorized as deflagrations, detonations, and thermal explosions.

C.2.1 Container Failure. When a container is pressurized beyond its burst strength, it can violently tear asunder (explode). A container failure can produce subsonic, sonic, or supersonic shock waves, depending on the cause of the internal pressure.

C.2.1.1 The energy released by failure of a vessel containing a gas or liquid is the sum of the energy of pressurization of the fluid and the strain energy in the vessel walls due to pressure-induced deformation.

C.2.1.2 In pressurized gas systems, the energy in the compressed gas represents a large proportion of the total energy released in a vessel rupture, whereas in pressurized liquid systems, the strain energy in the container walls represents the more significant portion of the total explosion energy available, especially in high-pressure systems.

Table B.2.5 Degrees of Instability Hazards

Degree of Hazard	Criteria
4 — Materials that in themselves are readily capable of detonation or explosive decomposition or explosive reaction at normal temperatures and pressures.	Materials that are sensitive to localized thermal or mechanical shock at normal temperatures and pressures Materials that have an instantaneous power density (product of heat of reaction and reaction rate) at 250°C (482°F) of 1000 W/mL or greater
3 — Materials that in themselves are capable of detonation or explosive decomposition or explosive reaction, but that require a strong initiating source or that must be heated under confinement before initiation.	Materials that have an instantaneous power density (product of heat of reaction and reaction rate) at 250°C (482°F) at or above 100 W/mL and below 1000 W/mL Materials that are sensitive to thermal or mechanical shock at elevated temperatures and pressures
2 — Materials that readily undergo violent chemical change at elevated temperatures and pressures.	Materials that have an instantaneous power density (product of heat of reaction and reaction rate) at 250°C (482°F) at or above 10 W/mL and below 100 W/mL
1 — Materials that in themselves are normally stable, but that can become unstable at elevated temperatures and pressures.	Materials that have an instantaneous power density (product of heat of reaction and reaction rate) at 250°C (482°F) at or above 0.01 W/mL and below 10 W/mL
0 — Materials that in themselves are normally stable, even under fire conditions.	Materials that have an instantaneous power density (product of heat of reaction and reaction rate) at 250°C (482°F) below 0.01 W/mL Materials that do not exhibit an exotherm at temperatures less than or equal to 500°C (932°F) when tested by differential scanning calorimetry

[**704:**Table 7.2]

C.2.1.3 Small-volume liquid systems pressurized to over 34,500 kPa (5000 psi), large-volume systems at low pressures, or systems contained by vessels made of materials that exhibit high elasticity should be evaluated for energy release potential under accident conditions. This does not imply that nonelastic materials of construction are preferred. Materials with predictable failure modes are preferred.

C.2.1.4 Liquid systems containing entrained air or gas store more potential energy and are, therefore, more hazardous than totally liquid systems because the gas becomes the driving force behind the liquid.

C.2.1.5 For gas-pressurized liquid systems, such as nitrogen over oil, an evaluation of the explosion energy should be made for both the lowest and highest possible liquid levels.

C.2.1.6 For two-phase systems, such as carbon dioxide, an energy evaluation should be made for the entire system in the gas phase, and the expansion of the maximum available liquid to the gas phase should then be considered.

C.2.2 Deflagration. A deflagration is propagation of a combustion zone at a velocity that is less than the speed of sound in the unreacted medium. [**68**, 2007]

C.2.2.1 The reaction rate is proportional to the increasing pressure of the reaction. A deflagration can, under some conditions, accelerate and build into a detonation.

C.2.2.2 The deflagration-to-detonation transition (D-D-T) is influenced by confinement containment that allows compression waves to advance and create higher pressures that continue to increase the deflagration rates. This is commonly called *pressure piling*.

C.2.3 Detonation.

C.2.3.1 A detonation is propagation of a combustion zone at a velocity that is greater than the speed of sound in the unreacted medium. [**68**, 2007]

C.2.3.2 A detonation causes a high-pressure shock wave to propagate outwardly, through the surrounding environment, at velocities above the speed of sound.

C.2.4 Thermal Explosion. A thermal explosion is a self-accelerating exothermic decomposition that occurs throughout the entire mass, with no separate, distinct reaction zone.

C.2.4.1 A thermal explosion can accelerate into a detonation.

C.2.4.2 The peak pressure and rate of pressure rise in a thermal explosion are directly proportional to the amount of material undergoing reaction per unit volume of the container. This is quite unlike gas or vapor explosions, where the loading density is normally fixed by the combustible mixture at one atmosphere. The Frank-Kamenetskii theory is useful in evaluating the critical mass in the thermal explosion of solids.

C.3 Effects of Explosions.

C.3.1 Personnel Exposure. Personnel exposed to the effects of an explosion are susceptible to injury from the following:

(1) Missiles and explosion-dispersed materials
(2) Thermal and corrosive burns
(3) Inhalation of explosion products
(4) Overpressure, including incident, reflection-reinforced incident, and sustained overpressure
(5) Body blowdown and whole-body displacement

Injuries from missiles and explosion-dispersed materials, burns, and inhalation of toxic gases account for the majority of injuries related to small explosions. Approximation of physiological damage due to explosions is given in Table C.3.1(a) and Table C.3.1(b).

C.3.2 Damage to Structural Elements. The potential for damage to high-value buildings and equipment also warrants special consideration. Failure of building components should not be overlooked as a source of injury to personnel.

C.3.2.1 Where the incident impulse is reinforced by reflection, as will be the case in large explosions within or near structures, the incident peak pressures for given damage are substantially lowered. The reflected pressure might be from 2 to 19 times greater than the incident pressure, depending on the magnitude of the incident pressure and the distance from reflecting surfaces. However, when a small explosion located more than a few inches from a reflecting surface has a TNT equivalence of less than 100 g (3.5 oz), the reinforcement phenomenon is negligible because of the rapid decay of both the incident pressure wave and the reflected pressure wave with distance.

C.3.2.2 Thermal explosions and deflagrations having impulses with rates of pressure rise greater than 20 milliseconds require peak pressures approximately three times those of detonations in order to produce similar damage.

C.3.2.3 A sustained overpressure will result when a large explosion occurs in a building with few openings or inadequate explosion venting. This sustained overpressure is more damaging than a short duration explosion of equivalent rate of pressure rise and peak pressure. Explosions with TNT equivalencies of less than 100 g (3.5 oz) would not be expected to create significant sustained overpressures, except in small enclosures. (For small explosions, burns, inhalation of toxic gases, and missile injuries usually exceed blast wave injuries.)

C.4 Hazard Analysis.

C.4.1 The determination of the degree of hazard presented by a specific operation is a matter of judgment. An explosion hazard should be evaluated in terms of likelihood, severity, and the consequences of an explosion, as well as the protection required to substantially reduce the hazard. A review of the explosion hazard analysis by an appropriate level of management is recommended.

C.4.2 The severity of an explosion is measured in terms of the rate of pressure rise, peak explosion pressure, impulse, duration of the overpressure, dynamic pressure, velocity of the propagating pressure wave, and residual overpressures. The effects of an explosion within an enclosure, such as a laboratory hood, laboratory work area, or laboratory unit can be far more severe than the effects of a similar explosion in an open space. Of primary importance is the missile hazard. Some explosions, such as in overpressurized lightweight glassware, can generate pressure waves that, in themselves, do not endanger personnel, but the resulting fragments can blind, otherwise injure, or kill the experimenter. An explosion that develops pressures sufficient to endanger personnel in a laboratory work area usually will present a serious missile hazard. Consideration of missile hazards should include primary missiles from the vessel in which the explosion originates, secondary missiles accelerated by the expanding blast wave, and the mass, shape, and velocity of the missiles. It should be noted that an improperly anchored or inadequately designed shield also can become a missile. The possibility of flames and dispersion of hot, corrosive, or toxic materials likewise should be considered.

Table C.3.1(a) Blast Effects from Detonations

Blast Effect	Range (ft) for Indicated Explosive Yield (TNT Equivalent)				Criteria	
	0.1 g	1.0 g	10 g	100 g		
1% eardrum rupture	1.1	2.4	5.2	11	23.5 kPa	$(P_i = 3.4 \text{ psi})$
50% eardrum rupture	0.47	1.0	2.2	4.7	110 kPa	$(P_i = 16 \text{ psi})$
No blowdown	0.31	1.3	6.9	~30	57 kPa · msec	$(I_i + I_q = 1.25 \text{ psi} \cdot \text{msec})$
					0.9 m/sec	$(V_{max} = 0.3 \text{ ft/sec})$
50% blowdown	<0.1	0.29	1.1	4.1	57 kPa · msec	$(I_i + I_q = 8.3 \text{ psi} \cdot \text{msec})$
					0.6 m/sec	$V_{max} = 2.0 \text{ ft/sec}$
1% serious displacement injury	<0.1	<0.2	<0.5	~1.1	373 kPa · msec	$(I_i + I_q = 54 \text{ psi} \cdot \text{msec})$
					V_{max} 4 msec	$(V_{max} = 13 \text{ ft/sec})$
Threshold lung hemorrhage	<0.1	<0.2	0.5	1.8	180 kPa · msec	$(I_i + I_q = 26 \text{ psi} \cdot \text{msec})$
Severe lung hemorrhage	<0.1	<0.2	<0.5	~1.1	360 kPa · msec	$(I_i + I_q = 52 \text{ psi} \cdot \text{msec})$
1% mortality	<0.1	<0.2	<0.5	<1	590 kPa · msec	$(I_i + I_q = 85 \text{ psi} \cdot \text{msec})$
50% mortality	<0.1	<0.2	<0.5	<1	900 kPa · msec	$(I_i + I_q = 130 \text{ psi} \cdot \text{msec})$
50% large 1.5 m² to 2.3 m² (16 ft² to 25 ft²) windows broken	0.26	1.1	5.7	~ 30	21 kPa · msec	$(I_r = 3 \text{ psi} \cdot \text{msec})$
50% small 0.12 m² to 0.56 m² (1.3 ft² to 6 ft²) windows broken	0.17	0.40	1.9	9.9	55 kPa · msec	$(I_r = 8 \text{ psi} \cdot \text{msec})$

For U.S. customary units, 1 g = 0.04 oz; 1 m = 3.3 ft.

P_i = peak incident overpressure kPa (psi)

V_{max} = maximum translational velocity for an initially standing man m/sec (ft/sec)

I_i = impulse in the incident wave kPa · msec (psi · msec)

I_q = dynamic pressure impulse in the incident wave kPa · msec (psi · msec)

I_r = impulse in the incident wave upon reflection against a surface perpendicular to its path of travel kPa · msec (psi · msec)

Note: The overpressure-distance curves of thermal explosions and deflagrations do not match those of TNT detonations. Nondetonation explosions have lower overpressures in close for comparable energy releases but carry higher overpressures to greater distances. The critical factor is impulse. Impulse is the maximum incident overpressure (psi) multiplied by the pulse duration (msec).

Table C.3.1(b) Criteria for Estimating Missile Injuries

Kind of Missile	Critical Organ or Event	Related Impact Velocity	
		m/sec	ft/sec
Nonpenetrating 4.5 kg (10 lb) object	Cerebral concussion:		
	Threshold	4.6	15
	Skull fracture:		
	Threshold	4.6	15
	Near 100%	7.0	23
Penetrating* 10 g (0.35 oz) glass fragments	Skin laceration:		
	Threshold	15	50
	Serious wounds:		
	Threshold	30	100
	50%	55	180
	100%	91	300

*Eye damage, lethality, or paralysis can result from penetrating missiles at relatively low velocities striking eyes, major blood vessels, major nerve centers, or vital organs.

C.4.3 The likelihood of an explosion is estimated by considering such factors as the properties of the reactants; history of the reaction based on literature search, and so forth; possible intermediates and reaction products; pressure, volume, stored energy, design integrity, and safety factors of reaction vessels; pressure relief provisions, in the case of pressure vessels; and explosive limits, quantities, oxygen enrichment, and so forth, of flammable gases or vapors. The term *likelihood*, rather than *probability*, is used to describe an estimated event frequency based on experience, knowledge, or intuitive reasoning, rather than on statistical data. In general, there will be insufficient data to develop mathematical probabilities.

C.4.4 The consequences of an explosion can be estimated by considering the interactions of the explosion with personnel, equipment, and building components at varying distances from the center of the explosion. This analysis should include the following:

(1) Numbers and locations of personnel
(2) Injury and fatality potentials
(3) Repair or replacement cost of equipment
(4) Ability of the building or room or equipment to withstand the explosion and the cost to restore the facility and equipment
(5) Adverse impact on research and development and business interruption costs as a result of loss of use of the facility

C.4.5 Figure C.4.5 provides guidance on distinguishing between high-pressure and low-pressure reactions.

Items in C.4.5.1 through C.4.5.3 apply to the classification of reactions in vessels as either high pressure or low pressure.

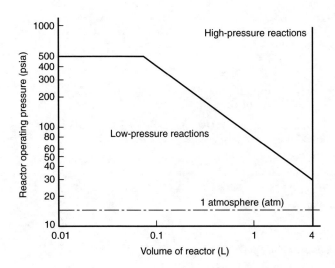

FIGURE C.4.5 Pressure Classification of Reactions.

C.4.5.1 Reactions that produce pressures below the curve in Figure C.4.5 are classified as low-pressure reactions.

An exception to this paragraph follows: Experimental reactions involving materials that are known to be inherently unstable, such as reactions with acetylenic compounds and certain oxidations, such as halogenations or nitrations, should be considered high-pressure reactions, even though they might fall below the curve in Figure C.4.5.

C.4.5.2 Reactions that produce pressures above the curve in Figure C.4.5 should be classified as high-pressure reactions.

An exception to this paragraph follows: Routine reactions where pressures and temperatures are expected between certain predetermined limits based on long experience or routine work might be considered low-pressure reactions, if the reaction vessel is built of suitable materials, has an adequate safety factor, and is provided with pressure relief in the form of a properly designed safety relief valve or a rupture disc that discharges to a safe location.

C.4.5.3 Items C.4.5.3.1 through C.4.5.3.4 contain recommendations for protecting against explosion hazards of reactions conducted above atmospheric pressures.

C.4.5.3.1 High-pressure experimental reactions should be conducted behind a substantial fixed barricade that is capable of withstanding the expected lateral forces. The barricade should be firmly supported at top and bottom to take these forces. At least one wall should be provided with explosion venting directed to a safe location. *(See NFPA 68, Standard on Explosion Protection by Deflagration Venting.)*

C.4.5.3.2 Reaction vessels should be built of suitable materials of construction and should have an adequate safety factor.

C.4.5.3.3 All reaction vessels should be provided with a pressure relief valve or a rupture disc.

C.4.5.3.4 Low-pressure reactions should be conducted in or behind portable barricades.

C.5 Explosion Hazard Protection.

C.5.1 It is important to remember that a conventional laboratory hood is not designed to provide explosion protection.

C.5.2 The design of explosion hazard protection measures should be based on the following considerations:

(1) Blast effects, as follows:
   (a) Impulse
   (b) Rate and duration of pressure rise
   (c) Peak pressure
   (d) Duration of overpressure
   (e) Velocity of the propagating pressure wave
   (f) Residual overpressure and underpressure
(2) Missiles, as follows:
   (a) Physical properties of the material
   (b) Mass
   (c) Shape
   (d) Velocity

C.5.3 Protection can be provided by one or more of the following methods:

(1) Providing special preventive or protective measures (such as explosion suppression, high-speed fire detection with deluge sprinklers, explosion venting directed to a safe location, or explosion-resistant enclosures) for reactions, equipment, or the reactants themselves
(2) Using remote control to minimize personnel exposure
(3) Conducting experiments in a detached or isolated building, or outdoors
(4) Providing explosion-resistant walls or barricades around the laboratory
(5) Limiting the quantities of flammable or reactive chemicals used in or exposed by the experiments
(6) Limiting the quantities of reactants of unknown characteristics to fractional gram amounts until the properties of intermediate and final products are well established
(7) Providing sufficient explosion venting in outside walls to maintain the integrity of the walls separating the hazardous laboratory work area from adjacent areas (Inside walls should be of explosion-resistant construction.)
(8) Disallowing the use of explosion hazard areas for other nonexplosion hazard uses
(9) Locating offices, conference rooms, lunchrooms, and so forth, remote from the explosion hazard area

C.5.4 Explosion-Resistant Hoods and Shields. Laboratory personnel can be protected by specially designed explosion-resistant hoods or shields for TNT equivalencies up to 1.0 g (0.04 oz). For slightly greater TNT equivalencies, specially designed hoods provided with explosion venting are required. For TNT equivalencies greater than 2.0 g (0.07 oz), explosion-resistant construction, isolation, or other protective methods should be used.

C.5.4.1 Conventional laboratory hoods are not designed to provide explosion protection.

C.5.4.2 When explosion-resistant hoods or shields are used, they should be designed, located, supported, and anchored so as to do the following:

(1) Withstand the effects of the explosion
(2) Vent overpressures, injurious substances, flames, and heat to a safe location
(3) Contain missiles and fragments
(4) Prevent the formation of secondary missiles caused by failure of hood or shield components

C.5.4.3 Commercially available explosion shields should be evaluated against the criteria of C.5.4.2 for the specific hazard.

C.5.4.4 Mild steel plate offers several advantages for hood and shield construction. It is economical, easy to fabricate, and tends to fail, at least initially, by bending and tearing, rather than by spalling, shattering, or splintering.

The use of mirrors or closed-circuit television to view the experiments allows the use of nontransparent shields without hampering the experimenter.

C.5.4.5 When transparent shields are necessary for viewing purposes, the most common materials used are safety glass, wire-reinforced glass, and acrylic or polycarbonate plastic. Each of these materials, although providing some missile penetration resistance, has a distinct failure mode.

Glass shields tend to fragment into shards and to spall on the side away from the explosion. Plastics tend to fail by cracking and breaking into distinct pieces. Also, plastics can lose strength with age, exposure to reactants, or mechanical action. Polycarbonates exhibit superior toughness compared to acrylics.

Glass panels and plastic composite panels (safety glass backed with polycarbonate, with the safety glass toward the explosion hazard) have been suggested as an improved shield design. The glass blunts sharp missiles, and the polycarbonate contains any glass shards and provides additional resistance to the impulse load.

C.5.5 Explosion-Resistant Construction. As explained in C.5.4, explosion-resistant construction can be required for TNT equivalencies greater than 2.0 g (0.07 oz). Explosion-resistant construction should be designed based on the anticipated blast wave, defined in terms of peak impulse pressure and pulse duration, and the worst-case expected missile hazard, in terms of material, mass, shape, and velocity. Missile velocities of 305 m/sec to 1220 m/sec (1000 ft/sec to 4000 ft/sec) normally can be expected.

C.5.5.1 The response of a wall to an explosive shock is a function of the pressure applied and of the time period over which the pressure is applied. The pressure-time product is known as impulse.

Detonations of small quantities of explosive materials usually involve very short periods of time (tenths of milliseconds) and high average pressure.

Gaseous deflagrations usually involve longer time periods and low average pressures.

C.5.5.2 Information on design of explosion-resistant walls and barricades can be obtained from references in Annex G.

C.5.6 Explosion Venting. Peak pressure and impulse loadings resulting from deflagrations (not detonations) can be significantly reduced by adequate explosion venting. *(See NFPA 68, Standard on Explosion Protection by Deflagration Venting, for information on calculating required vent areas.)*

C.5.6.1 Explosion vents should be designed and located so that fragments will not strike occupied buildings or areas where personnel could be located. Blast mats, energy-absorbing barriers, or earthen berms can be used to interrupt the flight of fragments.

C.5.6.2 An air blast, unlike a missile, is not interrupted by an obstacle in its line of travel. Instead, the blast wave will diffract around the obstacle and, except for slight energy losses, is essentially fully reconstituted within five to six obstacle dimensions beyond the obstacle. However, in the case of a small [TNT equivalence of 100 g (3.5 oz) or less] explosion, the wave decay with distance can more than offset the reinforcement phenomena.

Annex D Supplementary Information on the Concept of the Laboratory Unit

This annex is not a part of the requirements of this NFPA document but is included for informational purposes only.

D.1 Definitions. The following terms, defined in Section 3.3 of this standard, are essential to the understanding of this annex:

(1) Laboratory
(2) Laboratory work area
(3) Laboratory unit
(4) Laboratory unit separation

D.2 Basic Concepts.

D.2.1 The concept of a laboratory is too nebulous to be used for establishing requirements for fire protection. The term *laboratory* has too many differing and conflicting interpretations.

D.2.2 The requirements of this standard are based on the concept of the laboratory work area and the laboratory unit.

D.2.3 The term *laboratory work area* applies to any area that serves the purpose of a laboratory. It need not be enclosed. If enclosed, it need not constitute an individual fire area. If the boundaries of a laboratory work area do coincide with fire separation from adjacent areas, then that laboratory work area is also a laboratory unit and is more properly defined as such.

D.2.4 The term *laboratory unit* is meant to comprise any separate fire area that contains one or more laboratory work areas. The fire resistance rating of the separation between the laboratory unit and adjacent areas, or below, is dependent on the size of the unit; its class, according to Chapter 4; amounts of flammable and combustible liquids; and the presence, or lack, of an automatic extinguishing system.

Consider the laboratory unit shown in Figure D.2.4(a); the laboratory unit is totally enclosed by a fire separation. This

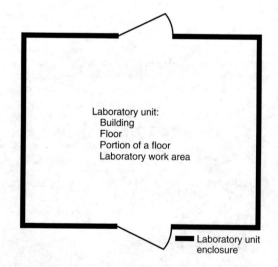

FIGURE D.2.4(a) Laboratory Unit.

laboratory unit can be an entire building, just one floor of a building, or only a portion of one floor of a building.

Figure D.2.4(b) shows the same laboratory unit, but with more details added. Note that, by adding work benches and a desk, the laboratory unit is now divided into three distinct work areas and a non-laboratory area, namely the office area. Further, although there is no physical separation between these four areas, other than the furniture, they are still separate and distinct and can be so treated. For example, smoking might be allowed at the desk but not in the work areas. Or, the work area at the upper left quadrant might be restricted to very simple, nonhazardous routines.

In Figure D.2.4(c), the work areas and the office area shown in Figure D.2.4(b) are separated by physical barriers, most likely the steel panel and glass partitions commonly used in laboratory

partitioning. Although the partitions have no fire resistance rating, they still afford a minimal degree of protection.

Figure D.2.4(d) shows an entirely different situation. The corridor is now a required means of exit access. Therefore, it should be separated from the laboratory units by fire-rated construction. This converts the single laboratory unit into two laboratory units: one having two separate workrooms and one having a workroom and an office.

Figure D.2.4(e) shows how a non-laboratory area and a Class C laboratory unit are separated both from each other and from an exit passageway. On the other side of the means of exit access, the two laboratory work areas of Figure D.2.4(e) are now separated by a fire partition into two laboratory units of differing class.

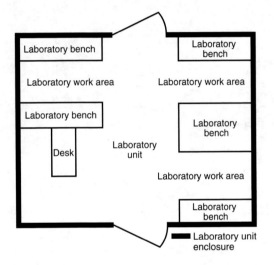

FIGURE D.2.4(b) Laboratory Unit Without Partitioning.

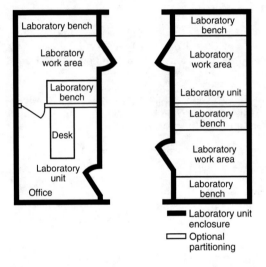

FIGURE D.2.4(d) Laboratory Units Separated by an Exit Passageway.

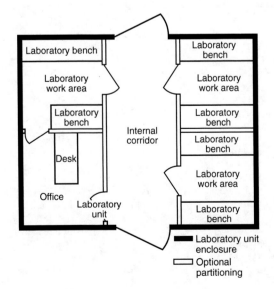

FIGURE D.2.4(c) Laboratory Unit with Optional Partitioning.

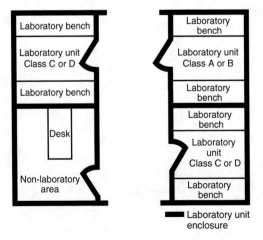

FIGURE D.2.4(e) Separation of Laboratory Units and Non-Laboratory Areas.

D.3 Factors Affecting Laboratory Unit Fire Hazard Classification.

D.3.1 The primary factor in determining laboratory unit fire hazard classification is the quantity of Class I, Class II, and Class IIIA liquids, as defined in Annex B. A survey of flammable liquid usage and storage in any particular laboratory unit should identify the quantities of Class I liquids alone and Class I, Class II, and Class IIIA liquids combined. The survey should differentiate between the total amounts present and the amounts that are not stored in approved storage cabinets or safety cans. Further, flammable and combustible liquids inside liquid storage areas meeting the requirements of NFPA 30, *Flammable and Combustible Liquids Code*, are disregarded.

D.3.2 As shown in Table 10.1.1(a) and Table 10.1.1(b), maximum quantities of liquids differ by a factor of 2, depending on the presence or absence of automatic sprinkler protection (or equivalent protection).

D.3.3 The area of the laboratory unit will establish whether the quantities of Class I or Class I, Class II, and Class IIIA liquids actually present exceed the maximum limits specified in Table 10.1.1(a) and Table 10.1.1(b).

D.3.4 The construction requirements in Table 5.1.1 will establish whether the actual laboratory unit separation is proper for the laboratory unit fire hazard class and size.

D.4 Correcting Nonconforming Laboratory Units. The simplest, most obvious means of handling a noncomplying laboratory unit is to reduce the quantities of flammable and combustible liquids present. This could involve moving some liquids to an inside liquid storage area, but the chances are that a surprising amount of such liquids is not in frequent use and could even be of no value at all.

D.5 New Construction. In new construction, the laboratory designer should determine the intended use of each laboratory work area and intended storage levels of Class I, Class II, and Class IIIA liquids. Then, based on this information and desired space requirements, the laboratory designer can determine the probable laboratory unit fire hazard class, allowable area (as specified in Table 5.1.1), and construction requirements.

Annex E Flammability Characteristics of Common Compressed and Liquefied Gases

This annex is not a part of the requirements of this NFPA document but is included for informational purposes only.

E.1 Table E.1 presents the flammability characteristics of common compressed and liquefied gases. The information provided in Table E.1 is not intended to be inclusive or exhaustive. Furthermore, practically all compressed and liquefied gases present varying health hazards to laboratory or emergency personnel. Therefore, the user is urged to seek additional information from reliable references to adequately assess the reactivity or toxicity of the material.

Table E.1 Flammability Characteristics of Common Compressed and Liquefied Gases

Gas	Flammable Limits (if flammable, percent by volume)	Reference Source
Acetylene	2.5–82	MGD
Allene*	1.5–11.5	MGD
Ammonia*	15–28	MGD
Arsine*	5.1–78	NIOSH
Boron Trichloride*	(a)	MGD
Boron Trifluoride	(a)	MGD
1,3-Butadiene*	2–12	627
n-Butane	1.6–8.4	325
iso-Butane*	1.8–8.4	325
1-Butene*	1.6–10	627, 325
2-Butene*	1.7–9.7	627
Carbon Monoxide	12.5–74	627
Carbonyl Chloride (Phosgene)*	(a)	NIOSH
Carbonyl Fluoride*	(a)	NIOSH
Carbonyl Sulfide*	12–29	325
Chlorine	(a)	NIOSH
Chlorine Dioxide*	(b)	NIOSH
Chlorine Trifluoride*	(a)	NIOSH
1-Chloro-1,1-di-fluoroethane*	9–14.8	MGD
Chlorotrifluoroethylene*	8.4–38.7	MGD
Cyanogen*	6–32	MGD
Cyanogen Chloride*	(a)	NIOSH
Cyclopropane*	2.4–10.4	MGD, 627
Deuterium	5–75	325
Diazomethane*	(b)	NIOSH
Diborane	0.8–98	325, 627
1,1-Difluoroethane*	3.7–18	MGD
1,1-Difluoroethylene*	5.5–21.3	MGD
Dimethyl Ether*	3.4–27	325, 627
2,2-Dimethyl Propane*	1.4–7.5	325, 627
Ethane*	3.0–12.5	MGD, 325, 627
Ethylacetylene*	(b)	MGD
Ethylamine*	3.5–14	325
Ethyl Chloride*	3.8–15.4	325
Ethylene	2.7–36	325, 627
Ethylene Oxide*	3–100	MGD
Fluorine	(a)	NIOSH
Formaldehyde	7–73	325
Germane	(b)	MGD
Hexafluoroacetone*	(a)	NIOSH
Hydrogen	4–75	325, 627
Hydrogen Bromide*	(a)	NIOSH
Hydrogen Chloride*	(a)	NIOSH
Hydrogen Cyanide*	5.6–40	325, 627
Hydrogen Fluoride*	(a)	NIOSH
Hydrogen Iodide*	(a)	MGD
Hydrogen Selenide*	(b)	NIOSH
Hydrogen Sulfide	4–44	325, 627
Ketene	(b)	NIOSH
Methane	5–15	325, 627
Methylacetylene* (Propyne)	2–11.1	325
Methylamine*	4.9–20.7	325
Methyl Bromide*	10–16	325

Table E.1 *Continued*

Gas	Flammable Limits (if flammable, percent by volume)	Reference Source
3-Methyl-1-butene*	1.5–9.1	325, 627
Methyl Chloride*	8.1–17.4	325
Methyl Fluoride*	(b)	MGD
Methyl Mercaptan*	3.9–21.8	325
2-Methylpropene	1.8–9.6	325, 627
Natural Gas	3.8/6.5–13/17	325
Nitric Oxide	(a)	NIOSH
Nitrogen Dioxide*	(a)	MGD
Nitrogen Trioxide*	(a)	MGD
Nitrogen Trifluoride*	(a)	MGD
Nitrosyl Chloride*	(a)	MGD
Oxygen	(a)	MGD
Oxygen Difluoride*	(a)	NIOSH
Ozone	(a)	NIOSH
iso-Pentane*	1.4–7.6	325
Perchloryl Fluoride*	(a)	NIOSH
Phosphine*	(c)	NIOSH
Propane*	2.1–9.5	325, 627
Propylene*	2.0–11.1	325
Selenium Hexafluoride	(a)	NIOSH
Silane	(c)	MGD
Silicon Tetrafluoride	(a)	MGD
Stibine	(b)	NIOSH
Sulfur Dioxide*	(a)	NIOSH
Sulfur Tetrafluoride*	(a)	NIOSH
Sulfuryl Fluoride*	(a)	NIOSH
Tetrafluoroethylene*	10/11–50/60	MGD, 325
Tetrafluorohydrazine*	(b)	MGD
Trimethylamine*	2–11.6	MGD, 325
Vinyl Bromide*	9–15	325
Vinyl Chloride*	3.6–33	325, 627
Vinyl Fluoride*	2.6–21.7	MGD
Vinyl Methyl Ether*	2.6–39	MGD

Notes:
(1) Flammable range:
  (a) Not flammable
  (b) Flammable, but range not reported
  (c) Spontaneously flammable
(2) Reference sources for flammable range:
325 — NFPA 325, *Guide to Fire Hazard Properties of Flammable Liquids, Gases, and Volatile Solids.* Although NFPA 325 has been officially withdrawn from the *National Fire Codes®*, the information is still available in NFPA's *Fire Protection Guide to Hazardous Materials.*
627 — U.S. Bureau of Mines Bulletin 627, *Flammability Characteristics of Combustible Gases and Vapors.*
MGD — *Matheson Gas Data Book.*
NIOSH — National Institute for Occupational Safety and Health, *Pocket Guide to Chemical Hazards.*
* Liquefied gas.

Annex F Safety Tips for Compressed Gas Users

This annex is not a part of the requirements of this NFPA document but is included for informational purposes only.

F.1 General Hazards. Thoroughly know the hazards of the gas you are using. All compressed gases have the pressure hazard, but a gas can also have more hazards; gases can be toxic, corrosive, flammable, asphyxiating, oxidizing, pyrophoric, and/or reactive. All these factors can impact the design of the system and how the gases are utilized.

F.2 Eye Protection. Always wear eye protection when working on or near compressed gas systems. Make it your job not to let anyone without eye protection into any area where compressed gases are used or stored.

F.3 Train Users. Never let anyone use or connect a cylinder to any system unless that person is trained and knowledgeable in the dangers of pressure, the chemical properties of the compressed gas, and the proper Compressed Gas Association (CGA) compressed gas fittings and connections.

F.4 Cylinder Identification. Do not use a compressed gas cylinder unless the cylinder is clearly marked or labeled with the cylinder's contents. Reject any cylinder that is unmarked or has conflicting markings or labels. Never rely on the color of the cylinder to identify the contents. If there is any conflict or doubt concerning the contents, do not use the cylinder. Return it to your vendor.

F.5 Cylinder Content. Be certain that the content of the cylinder is the correct product for use in the system to which you are connecting it.

F.6 Regulator Use. Never use a compressed gas cylinder without a pressure-reducing regulator or device that will safely reduce the cylinder pressure to the pressure of your system. Only use regulators that have both a high-pressure gauge and a low-pressure gauge. This allows you to monitor both the pressure in the compressed gas cylinder and the pressure in the system.

F.7 Pressure Gauge Use. As per ANSI B 40.1, *Pressure Gauges and Gauge Attachments,* never use a gauge above 75 percent of its maximum face reading. For example, a 20,700 kPa (3000 psi) system should use at least 27,600 kPa (4000 psi) gauges. If your system can achieve a maximum pressure of 517 kPa (75 psi), the gauge monitoring the system should be at least 690 kPa (100 psi). (Immediately replace any gauge whose pointer does not go back to its zero point when pressure is removed.)

F.8 Valves. Be sure the valve on the compressed gas cylinder and the pressure-reducing regulator you are using have the proper CGA connections for the pure gas (CGA V-1) or gas mixture (CGA V-7) you are using. NEVER USE AN ADAPTOR BETWEEN A CYLINDER AND A PRESSURE-REDUCING REGULATOR.

F.9 Proper Connection. Be certain the CGA connection(s) on the cylinder and the pressure-reducing regulator fit together properly without being too loose or too tight. Proper connections will go together smoothly. Never use excessive force to connect a CGA connection. NEVER USE AN AID, such as pipe dope or Teflon® tape, TO CONNECT A REGULATOR TO A CYLINDER.

F.10 Connections. Be certain that the pressure-reducing regulator you are using is compatible with the gas, and be certain that it is rated and marked for the maximum pressure rating of the CGA connection on the compressed gas cylinder valve you are attaching it to. All compressed gas cylinder connections can be found listed with their recommended gases and the maximum allowed pressures in CGA/ANSI V-1, *Standard for Compressed Gas Cylinder Valve Outlet and Inlet Connections.*

F.11 Regulator Compatibility. Never replace the CGA connection that the regulator manufacturer has put on a regulator with one for a different gas service. Only the regulator manufacturer or a trained service representative knows the gas compatibility of the regulator's internal design and can properly reclean the regulator.

F.12 Procedures. After attaching a pressure-reducing regulator to a compressed gas cylinder, do the following:

(1) Turn the regulator's adjustment screw out (counterclockwise) until it feels loose.

(2) Stand behind the cylinder with the valve outlet facing away from you.

(3) Observe the high-pressure gauge on the regulator from an angle; do not pressurize a gauge while looking directly at the glass or plastic faceplate.

(4) Open the valve handle on the compressed gas cylinder S-L-O-W-L-Y, until you hear the space between the cylinder valve gently fill the gas. (You can also watch the pressure rise on the high-pressure gauge. If you turned the regulator's adjustment screw back properly, there should be no gas flow out of the regulator or pressure rise on the low-pressure gauge.)

(5) If you are using a nontoxic, nonflammable gas, you can ensure purity by shutting off the cylinder valve and gently cracking the CGA connection at the cylinder valve. (Generally, three pressurizations with venting will ensure the interior of the connection has a clean, representative sample of the gas in the compressed gas cylinder. For toxic or flammable gases, you can purchase special venting regulators that can be safely vented to a fume hood or vented gas cabinet.)

(6) When you are ready to use the compressed gas cylinder, fully open the cylinder valve until you feel it stop. Then, close it one-quarter turn. (A fully open valve that has no play in it can confuse a person who is checking to see if it is open. Many accidents have been recorded by people trying to open a previously fully opened valve by using a large wrench.)

(7) Use the following practices on acetylene cylinders to allow quick closing of the valve in the event of an emergency:

(a) Open acetylene cylinder valves no more than one and one-half turns.

(b) Leave the wrench on the valve spindle when the cylinder is being used, if the acetylene cylinder has a T-wrench instead of a hand-wheel valve.

F.13 Pressure Relief. Make sure any system you are pressurizing (piping, manifolds, containers, etc.) that can be isolated or closed off has its own pressure-relief device. It is the user's responsibility to see that the system has proper pressure-relief device(s) built into it. Do not rely on the relief device on the compressed gas cylinder's regulator; it is not designed to protect downstream systems. This is very critical when cryogenic liquids are used. Pressure-relief discharge points should be vented to safe locations (not directed toward people or routed to safe locations for hazardous gases).

F.14 Cylinders Not in Use. Shut off cylinders that are not in use. Always have a cylinder cap on any cylinder that is being stored or is not in use.

F.15 Backflow Precautions. Use backflow check valves where flammable and oxidizing gases are connected to a common piece of equipment or where low- and high-pressure gases are connected to a common set of piping. Do not rely on a closed valve to prevent backflow.

F.16 Pressure Relief. The relief device on a cylinder of liquefied flammable gas (generally found on the cylinder valve) always should be in direct contact (communication) with the vapor space of the cylinder in both use and storage. Never lay a cylinder of liquefied flammable gas on its side unless it is so designed (and so marked) to allow that positioning, as in the case of propane cylinders for forklift trucks.

F.17 Protection of Cylinders in Use. Cylinders in use should be secured by a holder or device specifically designed to secure a cylinder. Never stand a single cylinder in an open area unsecured. Always protect cylinders from dangers of overhead hazards, high temperatures, and other sources of damage, such as vehicle traffic.

F.18 Moving Cylinders. Always use a cylinder cart to move large cylinders or specially designed cylinder holders to carry small cylinders. Never pick up a cylinder by its cap.

F.19 Refilling. Never refill a cylinder or use a cylinder for storing any material. If gas is accidentally forced back or sucked back into a cylinder, mark the cylinder well and inform your gas supplier. (Almost all recent deaths involving compressed gas cylinders occurred as users were putting gas back into cylinders and fillers at the compressed gas plants.)

F.20 Asphyxiation. Possibly the greatest hazard to a user of compressed gases — and especially users of cryogenic fluids — is asphyxiation. Remember that, except for oxygen and for air with at least 19.5 percent oxygen, ALL GAS IS AN ASPHYXIANT. Vent gas only into safe and properly ventilated locations outside the building or fume hood. EXPOSURE TO AN ATMOSPHERE THAT HAS 12 PERCENT OR LESS OXYGEN WILL BRING ABOUT UNCONSCIOUSNESS WITHOUT WARNING AND SO QUICKLY THAT THE INDIVIDUALS CANNOT HELP OR PROTECT THEMSELVES.

F.21 Cryogenic Gases. If you are transferring cryogenic gases inside or have equipment using cryogenic gases that vents anything more than a few cubic centimeters of gas per minute inside (i.e., not to a hood), you should have adequate 24-hour ventilation and install continuous oxygen meter(s)/monitor(s) with a "low oxygen" alarm.

Remember, all compressed gases are hazardous; understand those hazards completely and design your system accordingly. The major compressed gas vendors have the technical expertise available to support users. NEVER BECOME COMPLACENT WHEN USING A COMPRESSED GAS. Always respect the hazards and treat them accordingly.

Annex G   Informational References

G.1 Referenced Publications. The documents or portions thereof listed in this annex are referenced within the informational sections of this standard and are not part of the requirements of this document unless also listed in Chapter 2 for other reasons.

G.1.1 NFPA Publications. National Fire Protection Association, 1 Batterymarch Park, Quincy, MA 02169-7471.

NFPA 30, *Flammable and Combustible Liquids Code*, 2008 edition.

NFPA 68, *Standard on Explosion Protection by Deflagration Venting*, 2007 edition.

NFPA 69, *Standard on Explosion Prevention Systems*, 2008 edition.

NFPA 70®, *National Electrical Code®*, 2011 edition.

NFPA 77, *Recommended Practice on Static Electricity*, 2007 edition.

NFPA 86, *Standard for Ovens and Furnaces*, 2011 edition.

NFPA 90A, *Standard for the Installation of Air-Conditioning and Ventilating Systems*, 2009 edition.

NFPA 91, *Standard for Exhaust Systems for Air Conveying of Vapors, Gases, Mists, and Noncombustible Particulate Solids*, 2010 edition.

NFPA 92A, *Standard for Smoke-Control Systems Utilizing Barriers and Pressure Differences*, 2009 edition.

NFPA 101®, *Life Safety Code®*, 2009 edition.

NFPA 496, *Standard for Purged and Pressurized Enclosures for Electrical Equipment*, 2008 edition.

NFPA 704, *Standard System for the Identification of the Hazards of Materials for Emergency Response*, 2007 edition.

NFPA 801, *Standard for Fire Protection for Facilities Handling Radioactive Materials*, 2008 edition.

NFPA 1975, *Standard on Station/Work Uniforms for Emergency Services*, 2009 edition.

NFPA 5000®, *Building Construction and Safety Code®*, 2009 edition.

Fire Protection Guide to Hazardous Materials, 13th edition. 2001.

G.1.2 Other Publications.

G.1.2.1 AMCA Publication. Air Movement and Control Association International, Inc., 30 West University Drive, Arlington Heights, IL 60004-1893.

AMCA Standards Handbook 99-0401-86, *Classification for Spark Resistant Construction*, 1986.

G.1.2.2 ANSI Publications. American National Standards Institute, Inc., 25 West 43rd Street, 4th Floor, New York, NY 10036.

ANSI/AIHA Z9.5, *Laboratory Ventilation*, 2003.

ANSI/ASME A13.1, *Scheme for the Identification of Piping Systems*, 2007.

ANSI B40.1, *Pressure Gauges and Gauge Attachments*, 2005.

G.1.2.3 ASHRAE Publications. American Society of Heating, Refrigerating and Air Conditioning Engineers, Inc., 1791 Tullie Circle, NE, Atlanta, GA 30329-2305.

ASHRAE *Handbook of Fundamentals*, Chapter 14, "Airflow Around Buildings," 2007.

ASHRAE 110, *Method of Testing Performance of Laboratory Fume Hoods*, 1995.

G.1.2.4 ASME Publications. American Society of Mechanical Engineers, Three Park Avenue, New York, NY 10016-5990.

ASME *Boiler and Pressure Vessel Code*, Section VIII, "Rules for Construction of Pressure Vessels," Division 1, 2007.

ASME B31.1, *Power Piping*, 2007.

ASME B31.3, *Process Piping*, 2006.

G.1.2.5 ASTM Publications. ASTM International, 100 Barr Harbor Drive, P. O. Box C700, West Conshohocken, PA 19428-2959.

ASTM D 92, *Standard Test Method for Flash and Fire Points by Cleveland Open Cup*, 2005.

ASTM D 323, *Standard Method of Test for Vapor Pressure of Petroleum Products (Reid Method)*, 2006.

ASTM D 6668, *Standard Test Method for the Discrimination Between Flammability Ratings of F = 0 and F = 1*, 2006.

G.1.2.6 CGA Publications. Compressed Gas Association, 4221 Walney Road, 5th Floor, Chantilly, VA 20151-2923.

CGA Pamphlet P-1, *Safe Handling of Compressed Gases in Containers*, 8th edition, 2006.

CGA/ANSI V-1, *Standard for Compressed Gas Cylinder Valve Outlet and Inlet Connections*, 12th edition, 2005.

G.1.2.7 U.S. Government Publications. U.S. Government Printing Office, Washington, DC 20402.

Title 16, Code of Federal Regulations, Part 1500.44.

Title 49, Code of Federal Regulations, Part 173, Appendix H.

G.1.2.8 Other Publications. "An Investigation of Chemical Fume Hood Fire Protection Using Sprinkler and Water Mist Nozzles," Factory Mutual Research Corp., June 1999.

Bader, M., C. C. Phillips, T. R. Mueller, W. S. Underwood, and S. D. Whitson. "Returning Perchlorate-Contaminated Fume Hood Systems to Service, Part II: Disassembly, Decontamination, Disposal, and Analytical Procedures." *Applied Occupational and Environmental Hygiene*, Volume 14:369–375, 1999.

Bailey, J., Blair, D., Boada-Clista, L., Marsick, D., Quigley, D. R., Simmons, F., and Whyte, H. 2004(a). "Time Sensitive Chemicals (I): Misconceptions Leading to Incidents." *J. Chem. Health Safety* **11**(5): 14–17.

Bailey, J., Blair, D., Boada-Clista, L., Marsick, D., Quigley, D. R., Simmons, F., and Whyte, H. 2004(b). "Time Sensitive Chemicals (II): Their Identification, Chemistry and Management." *J. Chem. Health Safety* **11**(6): 17–24.

CRC *Handbook of Laboratory Safety*, Keith A. Furr, 4th edition, CRC Press, Chemical Rubber Company, Boca Raton, FL, 2000.

Cryogenic Fluids in the Laboratory, NSC Data Sheet 1-688-86, National Safety Council, 1986.

Frank-Kamenetskii, D. A. 1939. "Calculation of Thermal Explosion Limits." *U.S.S.R. Acta Physico-Chimica*, Volume 10, p. 365.

Matheson Gas Data Book, 7th edition, Matheson Co., East Rutherford, NJ, 2001.

Phillips, C. C., T. R. Mueller, B. Marwan, M. W. Haskew, J. B. Phillips, and D. O. Vick. "Returning Perchlorate-Contaminated Fume Hood Systems to Service, Part I: Survey, Sampling, and Analysis." *Applied Occupational and Environmental Hygiene*, **9**(7):503–509, July 1994.

Pocket Guide to Chemical Hazards, NIOSH, National Institute for Occupational Safety and Health, Washington, DC, September 2005.

Procedure for Certifying Laboratory Fume Hoods to Meet EPA Standards, Environmental Protection Agency, Safety, Health, and Environmental Management Division (3207A), Ariel Rios Bldg., 1200 Pennsylvania Ave., NW, Washington, DC 20406. Attn: Chief, Technical Support and Evaluation Branch.

Quigley, D. R., Simmons, F., Blair, D., Boada-Clista, L., Marsick, D., and Whyte, H. 2006. "Time Sensitive Chemicals (III): Stabilization and Treatment." *J. Chem. Health Safety* **13**(1): 24–29.

Schilt, A. A., and Erickson, L. E. 1981. *Perchloric Acid and Perchlorates*. Columbus, OH: The G. Frederick Smith Chemical Company.

Standard on Laboratory Fume Hoods (SEFA 1-2002), The Scientific Equipment and Furniture Association, 225 Reinekers, Suite 625, Alexandria, VA 22314, 2002.

UN Recommendations on the Transport of Dangerous Goods, Model Regulations, 15th rev. ed., 2005.

UN Recommendations on the Transport of Dangerous Goods, Manual of Tests and Criteria, 4th rev. ed., 2003.

U.S. Bureau of Mines Bulletin 627, *Flammability Characteristics of Combustible Gases and Vapors*, U.S. Bureau of Mines, Pittsburgh, PA, 1965.

G.2 Informational References. The following documents or portions thereof are listed here as informational resources only. They are not a part of the requirements of this document.

Allen, D. S. and P. Athens. 1968. "Influence of Explosion on Design." *Loss Prevention Manual — Volume 2.* New York: American Institute of Chemical Engineers.

ASTM D 5, *Standard Test Method for Penetration of Bituminous Materials,* 2006.

Brasie, W. C. and D. W. Simpson. 1968. "Guidelines for Estimating Explosion Damage." *Loss Prevention Manual — Volume 2.* New York: American Institute of Chemical Engineers.

Brinkley, S. R. 1969. "Determination of Explosion Yields." *Loss Prevention Manual — Volume 3.* New York: American Institute of Chemical Engineers.

CGA Handbook of Compressed Gases, 4th ed., 1999.

Cohen, E. 1968. "Prevention of and Protection Against Accidental Explosion of Munitions, Fuels, and Other Hazardous Mixtures." *New York Academy of Science Annals — Volume 152.* New York: New York Academy of Science.

Cote, A. E. 2008. *Fire Protection Handbook,* 20th edition. Quincy, MA: National Fire Protection Association.

Damon, E. G. et al. 1971. *Biodynamics of Air Blast,* Albuquerque, NM: Lovelace Biomedical and Environmental Research Institute.

Dobbs, N. et al. 1970. *New Concepts in the Design of Structures to Resist the Effects of Explosive-Toxic Detonations.* Dover, NJ: Picatinny Arsenal.

Gray, P. and P. R. Lee. 1967. *Thermal Explosion Theory,* New York: Elsevier Publishing Co.

Hartwigsen, C. 1971. *Shrapnel Containment Shields.* Albuquerque, NM: Sandia Laboratories.

Industrial Ventilation: A Manual of Recommended Practice for Design, 27th edition. 2010. Cincinnati, OH :American Conference of Governmental Industrial Hygienists (ACGIH).

Industrial Ventilation: A Manual of Recommended Practice for Operation and Maintenance, 27th edition, 2010.

JANNAF Propulsion Committee. 1971. "Chemical Propellant/Rocket Hazards." *General Safety Engineering Design Criteria,* Volume 2. Silver Springs, MD: Chemical Propulsion Information Agency.

Johnson, W. G. 1973. *The Management Oversight and Risk Tree.* Washington, DC: U.S. Government Printing Office.

Kinney, G. F. 1986. *Explosive Shocks in Air.* New York: The Macmillan Co.

Kinney, G. F. and G. S. Robert. 1972. *Pressure Rises in Internal Explosions.* Albuquerque, NM: University of New Mexico.

Klein, R. et al. 2004. "Solvent Vapor Concentrations Following Spills in Laboratory Chemical Hoods." Chemical Health and Safety, Washington, DC: American Chemical Society.

Lawrence, W. E. and E. E. Johnson. 1974. "Design for Limiting Explosion Damage." *Chemical Engineering,* Volume 81, No. 1, pp. 96–104, New York, NY: American Institute of Chemical Engineering (AIChE)..

Newmark, N. M. 1956. "An Engineering Approach to Blast Resistant Design." Transaction 121, Reston, VA: American Society of Civil Engineers.

NFPA 99, *Standard for Health Care Facilities,* 2005 edition.

Norris, C. H. et al. 1959. *Structural Design for Dynamic Loads.* New York: McGraw-Hill.

Prudent Practices in the Laboratory, National Research Council, National Academy Press, Washington, DC, 1995.

Polentz, L. M. "The Peril in Pressurized Liquids." *Design News,* September 6 and October 22, 1973.

Rogers, R. N. and J. Zinn. 1962. "Thermal Initiation of Explosives." *Journal of Physical Chemistry,* Volume 66, p. 2646.

Rules of the City of New York, Chapter 10, "Chemical Laboratories," Albany, NY: Lenz & Rieker, Inc., 1991.

Schram, P. J. and M. W. Earley. 1997. *Electrical Installations in Hazardous Locations.* Quincy, MA: National Fire Protection Association.

Smith, L. C. and M. J. Urizar. 1967. *Lightweight Safety Shields for Small Scale Operations Involving Explosives.* Los Alamos, NM: Los Alamos Scientific Laboratories.

Standard Specification for Laboratory Fume Hoods, Environmental Protection Agency, Washington, DC 20460, Attn: Chief, Facilities Engineering and Real Property Branch (PM-215).

G.3 References for Extracts in Informational Sections.

NFPA 30, *Flammable and Combustible Liquids Code,* 2008 edition.

NFPA 68, *Standard on Explosion Protection by Deflagration Venting,* 2007 edition.

NFPA 69, *Standard on Explosion Prevention Systems,* 2008 edition.

NFPA 99, *Standard for Health Care Facilities,* 2005 edition.

NFPA 704, *Standard System for the Identification of the Hazards of Materials for Emergency Response,* 2007 edition.

Index

Copyright © 2010 National Fire Protection Association. All Rights Reserved.

The copyright in this index is separate and distinct from the copyright in the document that it indexes. The licensing provisions set forth for the document are not applicable to this index. This index may not be reproduced in whole or in part by any means without the express written permission of NFPA.

Sequence of Events Leading to Issuance of an NFPA Committee Document

Step 1: Call for Proposals

•Proposed new Document or new edition of an existing Document is entered into one of two yearly revision cycles, and a Call for Proposals is published.

Step 2: Report on Proposals (ROP)

•Committee meets to act on Proposals, to develop its own Proposals, and to prepare its Report.
•Committee votes by written ballot on Proposals. If two-thirds approve, Report goes forward. Lacking two-thirds approval, Report returns to Committee.
•Report on Proposals (ROP) is published for public review and comment.

Step 3: Report on Comments (ROC)

•Committee meets to act on Public Comments to develop its own Comments, and to prepare its report.
•Committee votes by written ballot on Comments. If two-thirds approve, Report goes forward. Lacking two-thirds approval, Report returns to Committee.
•Report on Comments (ROC) is published for public review.

Step 4: Technical Report Session

•*"Notices of intent to make a motion"* are filed, are reviewed, and valid motions are certified for presentation at the Technical Report Session. ("Consent Documents" that have no certified motions bypass the Technical Report Session and proceed to the Standards Council for issuance.)
•NFPA membership meets each June at the Annual Meeting Technical Report Session and acts on Technical Committee Reports (ROP and ROC) for Documents with "certified amending motions."
•Committee(s) vote on any amendments to Report approved at NFPA Annual Membership Meeting.

Step 5: Standards Council Issuance

•Notification of intent to file an appeal to the Standards Council on Association action must be filed within 20 days of the NFPA Annual Membership Meeting.
•Standards Council decides, based on all evidence, whether or not to issue Document or to take other action, including hearing any appeals.

Committee Membership Classifications

The following classifications apply to Technical Committee members and represent their principal interest in the activity of the committee.

M   *Manufacturer:* A representative of a maker or marketer of a product, assembly, or system, or portion thereof, that is affected by the standard.
U   *User:* A representative of an entity that is subject to the provisions of the standard or that voluntarily uses the standard.
I/M   *Installer/Maintainer:* A representative of an entity that is in the business of installing or maintaining a product, assembly, or system affected by the standard.
L   *Labor:* A labor representative or employee concerned with safety in the workplace.
R/T   *Applied Research/Testing Laboratory:* A representative of an independent testing laboratory or independent applied research organization that promulgates and/or enforces standards.
E   *Enforcing Authority:* A representative of an agency or an organization that promulgates and/or enforces standards.
I   *Insurance:* A representative of an insurance company, broker, agent, bureau, or inspection agency.
C   *Consumer:* A person who is, or represents, the ultimate purchaser of a product, system, or service affected by the standard, but who is not included in the *User* classification.
SE   *Special Expert:* A person not representing any of the previous classifications, but who has a special expertise in the scope of the standard or portion thereof.

NOTES;
1. "Standard" connotes code, standard, recommended practice, or guide.
2. A representative includes an employee.
3. While these classifications will be used by the Standards Council to achieve a balance for Technical Committees, the Standards Council may determine that new classifications of members or unique interests need representation in order to foster the best possible committee deliberations on any project. In this connection, the Standards Council may make appointments as it deems appropriate in the public interest, such as the classification of "Utilities" in the National Electrical Code Committee.
4. Representatives of subsidiaries of any group are generally considered to have the same classification as the parent organization.

NFPA Document Proposal Form

NOTE: All Proposals must be received by 5:00 pm EST/EDST on the published Proposal Closing Date.

<table>
<tr><td>For further information on the standards-making process, please contact the Codes and Standards Administration at 617-984-7249 or visit www.nfpa.org/codes.

For technical assistance, please call NFPA at 1-800-344-3555.</td><td>FOR OFFICE USE ONLY

Log #: _____

Date Rec'd: _____</td></tr>
</table>

Please indicate in which format you wish to receive your ROP/ROC ☐ electronic ☐ paper ☒ download
(Note: If choosing the download option, you must view the ROP/ROC from our website; no copy will be sent to you.)

Date April 1, 200X   **Name** John J. Doe   **Tel. No.** 716-555-1234

Company Air Canada Pilot's Association   **Email**

Street Address 123 Summer Street Lane   **City** Lewiston   **State** NY   **Zip** 14092

***If you wish to receive a hard copy, a street address MUST be provided. Deliveries cannot be made to PO boxes.**

Please indicate organization represented (if any) _____

1. (a) NFPA Document Title National Fuel Gas Code   **NFPA No. & Year** 54, 200X Edition

(b) Section/Paragraph 3.3

2. Proposal Recommends (check one): ☐ new text   ☒ revised text   ☐ deleted text

3. Proposal (include proposed new or revised wording, or identification of wording to be deleted): [Note: Proposed text should be in legislative format; i.e., use underscore to denote wording to be inserted (inserted wording) and strike-through to denote wording to be deleted (deleted wording).]

Revise definition of effective ground-fault current path to read:

3.3.78 Effective Ground-Fault Current Path. An intentionally constructed, permanent, low impedance electrically conductive path designed and intended to carry underground electric fault current conditions from the point of a ground fault on a wiring system to the electrical supply source.

4. Statement of Problem and Substantiation for Proposal: (Note: State the problem that would be resolved by your recommendation; give the specific reason for your Proposal, including copies of tests, research papers, fire experience, etc. If more than 200 words, it may be abstracted for publication.)

Change uses proper electrical terms.

5. Copyright Assignment

(a) ☐ I am the author of the text or other material (such as illustrations, graphs) proposed in the Proposal.

(b) ☒ Some or all of the text or other material proposed in this Proposal was not authored by me. Its source is as follows: (please identify which material and provide complete information on its source)

ABC Co.

I hereby grant and assign to the NFPA all and full rights in copyright in this Proposal and understand that I acquire no rights in any publication of NFPA in which this Proposal in this or another similar or analogous form is used. Except to the extent that I do not have authority to make an assignment in materials that I have identified in (b) above, I hereby warrant that I am the author of this Proposal and that I have full power and authority to enter into this assignment.

Signature (Required) _____

PLEASE USE SEPARATE FORM FOR EACH PROPOSAL

Mail to: Secretary, Standards Council · National Fire Protection Association
1 Batterymarch Park · Quincy, MA 02169-7471 OR
Fax to: (617) 770-3500 OR Email to: proposals_comments@nfpa.org

6/09-B

NFPA Document Proposal Form

NOTE: All Proposals must be received by 5:00 pm EST/EDST on the published Proposal Closing Date.

For further information on the standards-making process, please contact the Codes and Standards Administration at 617-984-7249 or visit www.nfpa.org/codes.

For technical assistance, please call NFPA at 1-800-344-3555.

Please indicate in which format you wish to receive your ROP/ROC ☐ electronic ☐ paper ☐ download
(Note: If choosing the download option, you must view the ROP/ROC from our website; no copy will be sent to you.)

Date _____ Name _____ Tel. No. _____

Company _____ Email _____

Street Address _____ City _____ State _____ Zip _____

***If you wish to receive a hard copy, a street address MUST be provided. Deliveries cannot be made to PO boxes.*

Please indicate organization represented (if any) _____

1. (a) NFPA Document Title _____ NFPA No. & Year _____

   (b) Section/Paragraph _____

2. **Proposal Recommends (check one):** ☐ new text ☐ revised text ☐ deleted text

3. **Proposal (include proposed new or revised wording, or identification of wording to be deleted):** [Note: Proposed text should be in legislative format; i.e., use underscore to denote wording to be inserted (<u>inserted wording</u>) and strike-through to denote wording to be deleted (~~deleted wording~~).]

4. **Statement of Problem and Substantiation for Proposal:** (Note: State the problem that would be resolved by your recommendation; give the specific reason for your Proposal, including copies of tests, research papers, fire experience, etc. If more than 200 words, it may be abstracted for publication.)

5. Copyright Assignment

   (a) ☐ I am the author of the text or other material (such as illustrations, graphs) proposed in the Proposal.

   (b) ☐ Some or all of the text or other material proposed in this Proposal was not authored by me. Its source is as follows: (please identify which material and provide complete information on its source)

_____

I hereby grant and assign to the NFPA all and full rights in copyright in this Proposal and understand that I acquire no rights in any publication of NFPA in which this Proposal in this or another similar or analogous form is used. Except to the extent that I do not have authority to make an assignment in materials that I have identified in (b) above, I hereby warrant that I am the author of this Proposal and that I have full power and authority to enter into this assignment.

Signature (Required) _____

PLEASE USE SEPARATE FORM FOR EACH PROPOSAL

Mail to: Secretary, Standards Council · National Fire Protection Association
1 Batterymarch Park · Quincy, MA 02169-7471 OR
Fax to: (617) 770-3500 OR Email to: proposals_comments@nfpa.org

6/09-C